T0193948

Invisible **Chains,**
Visible **Threads**

ALICE KAYCEE

BALBOA.
PRESS
A DIVISION OF HAY HOUSE

Balboa Press books may be ordered through booksellers or by contacting:

Balboa Press
A Division of Hay House
1663 Liberty Drive
Bloomington, IN 47403
www.balboapress.com
1 (877) 407-4847

Because of the dynamic nature of the Internet, any web addresses or links contained in this book may have changed since publication and may no longer be valid. The views expressed in this work are solely those of the author and do not necessarily reflect the views of the publisher, and the publisher hereby disclaims any responsibility for them.

The author of this book does not dispense medical advice or prescribe the use of any technique as a form of treatment for physical, emotional, or medical problems without the advice of a physician, either directly or indirectly. The intent of the author is only to offer information of a general nature to help you in your quest for emotional and spiritual well-being. In the event you use any of the information in this book for yourself, which is your constitutional right, the author and the publisher assume no responsibility for your actions.

Any people depicted in stock imagery provided by Getty Images are models, and such images are being used for illustrative purposes only. Certain stock imagery © Getty Images.

Print information available on the last page.

ISBN: 978-1-9822-2875-0 (sc)
ISBN: 978-1-9822-2876-7 (e)

Balboa Press rev. date: 06/03/2019

TABLE OF CONTENTS

CHAPTER ONE

Grave

Not one tear fell at the grave.......

I stood silent, head bowed, the traditional grieving position. I opened my eyes to sneak a peek at all the others gathered. Besides me, my son and husband, the rest were devoted to their traditional burial regiment. Hands clasped with rosary beads in hand, black dresses. Men with black ties, appropriate silence and a priest who regurgitated The Our Father, followed by three Hail Mary's. He held his bible with precision along with a gold cross, of which he later adorned on the mahogany casket. I found myself repeating the age Old Catholic pray until I snickered slightly to myself. I stopped immediately. The crowd followed the direction of the priest by doing the sign of the cross. He uttered something in Latin and bowed his head.

The funeral director walked diligently towards my brothers and then towards me who was as far away as I could get from them and handed us each a bronze cross with Jesus in memory of our mother. An icon buried into the cost of the service I am sure. This was near the end of the service just before the casket was descended into the six foot depth of the earth, next to our father who had passed decades before. Had he still been alive, events would have been different. No doubt. I could hear my brothers sob, watching the noon sun reflect off of the glossy shine on the casket. This was the moment I understood that reflection. Clutched my bronze idol and silently thought I don't want this.

Zia Anna and Zio Domenic wandered off to visit other family grave sites after the traditional hugging and wailing, as did several others. There was the traditional kiss on both cheeks, a nod and wipe of tears. There was no need for Map Quest as each knew their designated paths. They have walked this cemetery many times. Some were disrespectful, walking over others graves to get to their loved ones. Odd how many profess doing the proper thing until something is important to them. Moral rules only apply to others, I guess?

My grandparents were across the gravel roadway that divided the sections with the older graves. I would have gone to say hello, but I didn't need to. Many of the guests today were scattered over there. The Italian community have difficulty with death I noticed, as I could hear the moans after the handkerchiefs came out. I am quite certain, in the older women's purses there is a memorial card with a Saint, or a picture of Father Pio. Perhaps, a small object from a deceased loved one who had passed decades ago. The rosary beads always got a kiss before being placed back into the purse. Maria Salmona was on her knees crying at her son's grave, grasping her rosary beads with some force. Her anger noted. He died of leukemia 30 years ago. Where had God been? She still wears black. I would pray for her, but I can't.

The weather held up though. No clouds, slight chill for an autumn day. It was funny watching some of the women getting their heels stuck in the grass. These were the young spouses of guests or family members with fiancés. Wearing stilettos to a funeral seemed odd, but fashionable apparently. The peculiar walk on the grass was a tad funny really, until I turned to my husband just after my own left heel sunk a centimetre or two and uttered "fuck". We both laughed. Actually so did our son. My heel was only an inch. Kyle was eighteen and attended a Public school until graduation. My husband Paul had been divorced with two sons. They are married now and out of province. Surprised lightening had not struck me yet. Zia Bianca prays for it I am sure. Some Catholics do that. Attend church, you know to monitor others. These moral rules get challenged often. Just like the Law. I was told by the police once that broken moral laws are not criminal. Ha, seems the two forms of law would be like the DNA. Two helixes connected. Woven like a fabric. I suppose everyone has a different style of fashion. Perhaps that's what the mirror is really for, to help us critique ourselves. So we can monitor if these Rules do apply to each and every one of us. After all we would be doomed to damnation would we not? That's what the nuns taught.

After all the hugging, condolences and words of advice such as, "God called her home, or, she has no more pain. Stay strong", were nothing more than redundant and insincere. I nodded gently to them, not wanting to upset them. Frightened for them that this is what they believe. I wanted to tap them on the shoulder with my bronze cross and tell them I was a Fairy, blessed with intelligence to erase the regurgitation of memes and unquestioned comments. But I couldn't. A lawsuit may ensue; after all, we are family. I bit my bottom lip and silently was wondering what the luncheon was going to be serving. I was getting hungry. I heard Kyle's stomach growl at the grave site. Bet you there would be alcohol. My brother was paying from my mother's estate. He is confused by the Moral rules. When our father died there was no alcohol. My mother thought it appropriate to just serve pop and water. She viewed it as a statement of respect to him. She didn't want people drunk or out of hand. She was always particular and prudent with her money. Makes me more certain wine will be just one of several items the bar will be serving. Not sure if his lawyer will be attending?

As the rows of cars were parting the cemetery, some of the guests were going towards the highway to their homes, others toward the luncheon at The Grotto. The Grotto is a members club that my father was affiliated with when he and his friends built it in the sixties. It was built out of necessity. Back in the fifties a group of immigrants landed in Evandale and had a hard time being accepted by the locals in their bars. They decided to construct a safe place for them to drink and play cards. They formed a membership and an Italian community flourished. At that time my father explained the Italians and Blacks were ranked the same. Both unaccepted. The French residents, who were rooted through generations here, didn't appreciate the competition. So the Grotto was a great place for the families that gathered over the years to celebrate weddings, christenings and religious festivals, undisturbed. Young girls met their spouses at one of these events. Many families orchestrated the union of their children to keep the custom and heritage intact. It was thought best to not divide cultures to secure traditional bias. The dialect they spoke was not understood by other Italians from different regions of Italy. The region many of the people who immigrated here came from a mountainous, farming community where education wasn't a requirement. They were good hearted people, driven by survival. My mother on the other hand, emigrated from a city. She had a grade six education. She felt displaced in this community. Sad that Alzheimer's stole her wise mind. This left it difficult to see who was stealing from her.

I was happy there was no limousine ride to the luncheon. The thought of being barricaded with my brothers and their spouses would not have fared well. Let's just say the bronze cross could have been forged into a mystical baton to ward off snakes. I could pretend to be St. Patrick. I learned this in Catholic School about saints. Later as an adult I learned about Mount Cashell. Perhaps my New Age philosophy had a place for discussion today?

Each carload carried its passengers over to the gathering. Our car load was small. My one brother Nick, was the third oldest. We accompanied his widow, Diane. See they had married during the tornado of family untruths. How I wished he hadn't left me alone to battle in court. But on the other hand, it has certainly made me strong. My mother didn't attend their wedding because she didn't know what an invitation even was at this point. I thought it was odd when she kept repeating herself, but my older brother Carmen, who never married said she was just fine. Nick and I weren't totally convinced.

His heart attack was probably a blessing. Too many people could have gone to prison. I knew too many of the officers already.

Others occupying our car were Paul, Kyle and I. I was the second oldest, Katia, my Married name Secord. I was lagging yards from the car at this point trying to brush the dirt from my heel. I met up with Steve, one of the Funeral Home aides. I liked him, he was Protestant. He knew of the tension within the family before the arrangements had been finalized. I know this because I told him. He had a charming whimsical personality and leaned into me just as we were all leaving the graveyard, and said, "want to hear something funny?" I did. "My Aunt Janice, no one liked. When my grandmother died my other aunt pushed her into the grave." He winked and walked away with some of the funeral props. I was amused and nodded wishing I could have seen that. Sad they were starting to back fill the grave. Steve couldn't make it to lunch.

Moments later we were in the car I started to share the story about Steve, until I was quickly interrupted. The rest of the car had begun the review of the Church Service an hour earlier. Paul jokingly chastised Diane as she needed to be pushed into the aisle way at St. Anthony's Church to get behind the casket at departure time. We could see how my brothers Carmen and Philip, the youngest, who were pallbearers, were led to the far side of the church after the casket had been rolled up the aisle way. I had been angry at Philip for deliberately leaving my family out of the procession. We were treated like casual attendees. I pounced at the opportunity to get behind the casket, when the priest started with the ritual bathing of the casket with incense; I adjusted my dress and whispered into Diane's ear, "if you're going to be part of this family, you'll have to keep up". I was positioned second in the pew. My brothers stared me down, angered that my family would be first. Diane was the second wife of only five years. She comes from a mindset of proper tradition where funerals are sacred. She was raised Methodist. Perhaps their rules are different? She is still learning that some people have ulterior motives. She doesn't have a lawyer.

Pulling away from the cemetery wasn't sad really. I glanced at the passing graves, knowing several of the names on the tombstones. Evandale was a small community of ten thousand. Chances were you crossed path with most of the community, or a member of their family at some point. I will admit I had to smile as we passed the Mausoleum in the extended part of St. Anthony's graveyard. This part borders the Protestant section, Stanton Hill. Odd only a gravel roadway divide the two sections. No fence, no wall. Unclear as why divisions exist in death? Thought death would be a neutral ground where communities could co-exist. The three story Mausoleum was adorned in bouquet of flowers in copper vases and crosses. Carved lettering with bronze details. My cross matched. I held it up as though we were connected by this sacred union because of our false idols. Almost thought I was in Rome. The opulence seemed wasteful, a projection of ornate beauty to appease a sad heart in a time of loss, diluting the real truth behind a loved ones passing. Stanton Hill just a stone throw away and their grounds had grave sites with less glamour. Sad really, that these divisions of understanding separated by a gravel road way will keep the community severed into eternity. Divisions of ideas masqueraded into rituals that become a commonplace format of devotion.

Sad really, that the Catholic Church has had to have legal representation over the years. Would have never thought there would ever be a need. Catholic school taught us the commandments. The nuns taught the required lesson for the curriculum. We had even been tested on this. I learned a lot. I once had a lawyer.

The crunch of the slow passing vehicles on the worn gravel seemed to echo in my mind. I heard the church bells chime in the distance. It was noon. Each day the church rings its bells at noon and at six. A habit they had gotten into for years now. A habit the town folk had become accustomed to. No matter what religion you followed.

Paul and Kyle sat in the front seat while Diane sat behind the front passenger. The music from Kyle's headphones was drowned out, only by me. Paul and Diane were in deep discussion about the church service. She seemed to be struggling with his explanations. Why she kept asking would someone act like this? I was hypnotically listening to each press of the rolling tires tamping the stones and dirt to the roadway behind us now, pondering the fact, that I just buried my mother. Distantly hearing Diane wondering, why?

I raised the cross in my right hand and stared at the pain in the clay Crucifixion. The bowed head and the droplets of bronze blood with feet nailed was the depiction of pain and sorrow. I felt numb at first but soon a sensation of anger crept upon me. Now I could hear the strong beats coming from Kyle's earphones. I found myself mesmerized by this clear day. No clouds, no wind. My grip on the cross was getting strong and a bit uncomfortable.......I remember it all. My heart pounding, as my blood pressure rose well beyond 120/80. The recall was not hidden, I just learned to pretend. One tear fell from my left eye. No one noticed. I was skilled at hiding things. I was now an orphan at fifty. The tires rolled with the procession of cars leaving the grave yard. I turned my head looking out the rear window. It needed cleaning. Didn't matter how vibrant the sun was. Dirt is dirt.

CHAPTER TWO

Counselling

Catherine welcomed me with a pleasant handshake. Her orderly office was reflective of how her thoughts and questions were posed. I always wanted to hug her because she was an integral piece in my healing. I however just knew that this is a breach of professional display. She was my counsellor now for five years. Our roles were pretty clear. Not like my brother's wife when she rubbed their lawyers back in court, after the judges ruling.

The neutral color palette of the office was actually inviting. The beige and grey was amplified by the bold artwork of oranges, yellow and red. The steel features of the furniture were strong and caught a slight reflection from the window above her desk. I loved that Catherine never used her desk in the thirty seven sessions we had, other than to write me a new appointment, depending on how the session went of course. Otherwise I would just call. Those days she always made an effort to squeeze me in. She found her purpose in life.

She sat to my left in a suede chair. A small table with only a box of tissue divided us. She always began with "so, anything to share today". Share was the new code word to unburden my psyche from the lies, distortions, and pretend role I had adopted. I learned that speaking the truth is a difficult script in your own life. When a script is carved into who you allowed yourself to be, there was no garment that could just be flicked off and a new identity had. No, this took deep thought. Deep introspection into the grooves of what formed this fifty year old. The beads of sweat and perspiration were usually an indication that I had retrieved some artefact that was stored and needed removal. Removal was never an easy process though. Guilt and shame often glue the internal tapestry that distorts the real face in the mirror. The DNA helix was spewed with a viral of confusion and self hate. My gentle demeanour had morphed into a handicapped soul. Unable to walk forward within my own life as my deeper being desperately wanted me to. My cells were stirring the debris like a Common Cold to flush the fragmentations out. I knew there would be a day that my medicine was a mirror. This box of tissue serves two purposes.

I started to gently rock back and forth not even realizing it. At this point there was no need for a tissue. I rocked and rocked. My eyes pierced upon the carpet. I was rocking saying nothing. I forgot that Catherine was even there. Rocking and thinking. Thinking and rocking. My lips were pressed tightly. Sounds were minimal beyond my heart and empty stomach. I gazed wanting to talk but I had not clutched the memory and feeling yet. I know the root was important. A firm mental grip and firm emotional readiness would restore an inner garden to its original beauty. The original beauty that that poets speak of and artists create. A beauty, my impartial true self knows me to be.

Sister Elizabeth was right in grade eight when she said "God doesn't make junk". I gave myself permission to believe this. When I dared to trust, I met Catherine. First I was interviewed by the Police. They have a department that is affiliated with her services. But I trusted.

Catherine had mentioned in an earlier session she would attend the court with me if charges are laid. I was grateful to her for that. I think she had a daughter. We hardly talked about her though. I heard her say, "Is it the dog"? I rocked. "Yes" I replied. This was my nineteen session. Gardening has become a passion.

There was a knock at the door which startled both of us. Quickly my mind had landed in present time and the kaleidoscope of uncomfortable memories ceased. My heart however was still intense. It was her secretary with an important message. Catherine politely excused herself and I remained looking through the window above her desk. I had yet to take a tissue but felt it wise to grab one before she came back. Her window was a stone throw away from my grade school that is unoccupied today. The population in Evandale has difficulty supporting three Catholic schools. Some days I miss the simplicity of childhood, or what I thought was simple. Recess was a welcoming break I remember, a favourite. Years later it was reported in our local paper two of our teachers had been charged with sexual assault. One was allowed to rotate from other schools for years on a promise he would stop this behaviour. The school board seemed impartial to abuse. I was fortunate I wasn't skinny or pretty back then. Thankfully I wasn't easy prey. I had suspicions of some girls from the volleyball team though. Sadly, popular girls stay among themselves. These secrets stay secure. That is until a parent finds a diary highlighting particulars. Blurring boundaries with the unpopular students seems almost sinful. In choir, we needed the entire class to perform to perfect our songs. But for popularity, unison was for those who drank and did drugs. They maintain a solid bond even after several of them had abortions. Not a bad thing I suppose, probably best to connect with someone who understands. Catherine has a tattoo over her left wrist.

Last I heard there were twenty five names attached to the charges. Twenty five names, all who made their first communions and their grade eight confirmations before moving on to high school. These rituals we were told were important to being Christian. Not sure where sex with a minor falls in the traditions? Perhaps catechism fell short? Someone misunderstood those commandments? Sister Elizabeth was a good role model though. She had values. She could hold a note when she taught music. I could hear her sing "God doesn't make junk". She made her own song. Never published, but it was popular to me.

I heard the turning of the knob and Catherine entered. She apologized with professionalism. There were others like myself who needed her services. Some needed a safety net in between appointments. Hope it wasn't a suicide?

"So where were we" she started, placing herself in her chair. "Yes", she said "you were sharing correct"? She tilted her head as though this was an acting cue to begin where I had left off. I left my childhood mirage and sat back into my chair. "Yes" I stated, "you asked me if it was about the dog"?

Feeling a bit more youthful after remembering my earlier school life I could feel a sense of a bounce in my spirit. My tissue was untorn, my ability to garden began. Sister Elizabeth was in my mind's eye. "Yes, in the first session with you, you asked me to depict a type of dog with each one of my family members. This exercise still troubles me to this day." "How so" asked Catherine?

"That junk yard dog. I can smell the garbage where I placed him in my mind". I responded.

"How," she said?

"Well, for instance I realize the vulnerable situation I was in and how intense the fear of him really was".

"Go on" she said.

"Well when you asked me to depict each one of my family, I thought this was going to be a playful session. You see I absolutely love dogs."

Catherine stated emphatically, "I gathered that. The first day you walked through that very door your sweatshirt had a face of a dog on it, remember"?

I nodded. I loved that shirt. Paul and the kids bought it for me one Christmas. It was a Labrador wearing a cowboy hat with a scarf around its neck.

Catherine then asked, "And who do you remember identifying

a Labrador with when I asked you to label each one of your family members?"

My eyes welled up with tears, it was my dad. I kept going between a Labrador and a Saint Bernard. Saint Bernard's are rescue dogs and unfortunately I chose the Labrador. My mother never told my dad. No one was coming to rescue me.

CHAPTER THREE

Leaving the Cemetery

Diane and Paul were joking around in the car. Diane mentioned that Americans do have lots of things that Canadians don't. Diane only became a Canadian after she married Nick. "Give me a for instance" stated Paul. They talked about the differences between Taxes and the difference in Healthcare. Then he started laughing and continued, both trying to out perform the others comments. "What's your take on guns? You're not going to say your pro gun laws are you?" This caught her off guard. She wasn't. Her sister was a supporter of the Right to Bear Arms. They were complete opposites. Funny isn't it how families are so different. How some DNA strands are woven with this tapestry of genetics but the personality that fuels the body are laced with so many different accent pieces. How does the universe spin this uniqueness? Neither one of them called the other to court. I was impressed. They had learned to agree to disagree. It was an interesting perspective really.

Kyle was starting to sing without realizing that we could hear him. Sadly his ability to hold a note, or sing the right words, was not one of his strengths.

"Would you stop," mentioned Paul.

Kyle hadn't heard. Paul elbowed him pointing to his own ears, giving a visual clue for Kyle to turn down the music. Kyle removed the ear buds and slight music could be heard from his device.

"What"? He questioned sincerely.

Paul leaned into him with one arm resting on the arm rest and said "your grandmother was just buried, do you think this is appropriate music?" Kyle took a second to reflect. He did just bury a grandmother, he knew that. He sadly never met his grandfather. His mom did speak highly of him but wasn't convinced had he been alive today he'd disapprove. See the swearing in the songs he was listening to were the words he really wanted to say, even if he didn't want to study law.

Hmmmmm, being disrespectful wasn't how he'd describe his music at all really. Considering the emotional turmoil he's experienced the last five years. He lost himself in thought, remembering his grandmother. His Nonna who wanted to be called Grandma, he remembered. The woman named Theresa Saldara. She was indeed his Nonna, but she became a Canadian citizen and wanted to fit in, so Grandma it was. Her silver hair and broken English was her trademark along with her short stature and hoop earrings. Always dressed in an apron and smelled of fresh bread. He loved how she retold stories of the Second World War. The danger she lived in, seemed so surreal. She shared how her role as a child was to help cook and do household chores, wondering if the bombs would destroy their city. She learned to bake bread at seven. It became a great distraction. Family was so very important to her. After all surviving the war she felt it was a blessing from God. Anytime she could baby sit Kyle was like giving her gold. It was such a precious joy. Being a widow can be lonely and isolating at times. Kyle loved sleeping over. She played Go Fish and War with a worn deck of cards. They belonged to his grandfather, Rocco. He heard stories of how they used to play Scooba together, an Italian card game which translates into Sweep. She was angered with herself for forgetting to put the cards in his grandfather's casket when he died. The joke was someone would have to remember when she died to put a deck in her casket, so they could play for eternity. Hmmmm" with repetitive nods was Kyle's response. "Hmmmm." followed by silence. Thinking of how he had been denied being a pallbearer or acknowledged today. As well as being stared down by an Uncle who had hardly visited his own mother. Feeling overlooked and robbed of his relationship with her. Cheated because a loving woman innocently lost her memory and was led to a lawyer's office to change her Will? "No, I'm good;" he said "easier to drown out the bullshit". He laughed. He had one dimple that complimented his cheek and put the ear phone back in. He knew there was a complaint at The Law Society on the lawyer's conduct. "Oh," he gestured taping his right index finger to his left wrist, "when's lunch?"

"Soon" Paul said, "once we get out of the graveyard we will take the back roads through the county to The Grotto".

Kyle put his right thumb up and did what any eighteen year old would and uttered under his breath, "cool". Little did he think that his grandmother would be a casualty of family war with a lawyer dropping the bomb?

Sadly no one put cards in the casket. I was the only one who knew this. I couldn't see her before she died because my brother's lawyer wrote me a letter. It stated that they would call the police if I tried to visit. I thought it proper not to disrupt the Nursing Home. The elderly have a right to enjoy the last days of their life, even if they didn't know where they were.

Her other children were crafty. Made it appear that they were a close knit family. Deception is an interesting craft really. Hollywood made many people wealthy. My problem was I knew the Commandments. Catholic school had been my weakness. I listened because I was scared of authority. I played the naive role in this stage performance. Best I could describe it was like being the tree in the backdrop of a live performance. Unfortunately my lawyer was not trained in live performance. He had been called to the Bar years ago and never perfected his craft. He came recommended, unfortunately.

I was denied talking at my mother's service. A sister in law who accused our mother of making her own children obese and not knowing how to administer first aide, had not earned the right to watch her own grandchildren, was now going to praise the very woman she avoided, odd really? Judgement cuts deep. What was the real motivation?

Thought it interesting though, that Steve's boss saw through this and I know this to be true, because I stormed out of the funeral home to talk to him. His brow was sweating a bit, but he confirmed it. She had been on the agenda to speak. People attending seemed confused when it was announced. Had my mother liked her, than it would have made sense? However, relatives had heard countless stories from Theresa's mouth for decades of how she disliked her. So this seemed odd. See I had to fire my lawyer, because he would have just let that go.

When Carmen was around, Kyle started noticing how his Grandma tended to shy away. Not quite as loving. Kyle would cut her grass and earn twenty bucks. Carmen would thoroughly critique the job before handing over the cash. Kyle thought it odd that he paid, when it was her money. She wasn't handling her finances as often. Oh well, Kyle knew his grandma was always afraid to be alone. Having an adult son living with you can cut down the loneliness. Well, when he wasn't at the Casino or Race track. Kyle used to come along to the doctor's appointments because Carmen was "working". Well that's what he called it. You know, gambling can be work you know. Health concerns were secondary. After all how long did a person really intend on living?

Diane shook her head. She lost Nick during this time frame with a massive heart attack. He had just made an appointment with Philip's lawyer to have Legal documents served on him. Took months to find him because his own brother didn't know where he lived. That's how close of a family we were. Philip had just gone through a fierce costly divorce that drained his bank account. The thought of another lawsuit had become overwhelming. The thought of losing more money became daunting. He knew the position was to fight a Guardianship Application. He and I were rooted in revealing the truth. You know the hidden truth. How monies that disappear from bank accounts for gambling purposes were manipulated. You know how an elderly person, who is lonely, is an easy prey for family to pounce on. Not always like the news reports. How strangers are always the bad guys. No, not at all, sometimes the criminals are fused within the genetic spine of a supposed family. Seemed odd that Philip was seeking this title after all I was already a Power of Attorney? Legal documents had been secured before his lawyer deemed her "incompetent"? Hmmmm odd really, a lawyer trying to find a way around changing an incapacitated woman's documents, seemed odd? But it wasn't really. See I had just gotten the courage to attend Evandale Police Department on a historic sexual assault. Phillip wasn't too pleased. The secret got out.

I had regretted not telling Nick when I was a kid. I did so when he was struggling with his own divorce nine years ago. Isn't it funny how upheaval can be a blessing? See, he faced his unhappiness. I faced the truth, head on. Philip killed Nick. Theresa didn't even know a son died. Carmen had to schedule time off from a poker tournament and Diane became the only member I chose to have as family with, besides, my own family. Nick's funeral was vibrant. He had lots of guests, just not his brothers. Diane wouldn't allow it.

Nick always had a no nonsensical approach to life. He was free-spirited and to say he was popular was an understatement. He loved sports, alcohol and a good party. But, abuse of this nature was not tolerated. He had a similar value system as our dad. In counselling I depicted him as a boxer. A loyal dog, whose face looked stern, he never wandered too far from a fight that made sense to him. Not the type to back down really.

Philip was a Rottweiler, chained to a fence in a junk yard. He was skilled to intimidate. He was not devoid of instincts. He was calculated in his manoeuvres, knowing when to pounce and being watchful helps to not getting caught. See when you're at a disadvantage with a physical illness that was yet to be diagnosed, you're more vulnerable. When you're naive that a sibling would even entertain an idea to pounce and hold down a sister, with a firm grip over her mouth while he firmly held her down with the strength of his athletic body, you are shocked. More so when you remember he closed the door before he chose to do this. Yes, closing that door. I just wanted to catch up on school work I had missed. Being home schooled was new for me. Nick said I could use his room because he had a nine inch television I could watch if I was bored. Nick and Philip shared a room. So when that door was closed, which had never happened before with me behind it, seemed unusual. It appeared to my mother unusual as well. When she opened it and glanced around the room and Philip was on his own bed seemed normal. See Philip had heard the footsteps down the hall and instinctively fled. My mother's eyes screamed confusion. In my heart I felt that she knew something had happened, but didn't say. That day I slammed that door in my fifteen year old heart wondering why?

My soul ached as the years crept on and I had not the courage to talk. Sharing with a friend seemed impossible. A relative that spoke English was even more impossible. Where does one turn? One hides, until they can't anymore.

Watching my parents being disrespected by Phillip became numbing. Adults who were bullied in their own home were disappointing to say the least. Where was an adult in charge? My mother's tears of anger and uncertainty on how to rectify her home to some normalcy were disappointing. I could hear her sob. I watched the tears trickle for months, believing at one point this was the moment, the moment to embrace my mother with a secret, a secret of which I knew in my heart that she already knew. I opened my mouth and gently said, "You know, I see the pain Phillip is causing you. How he doesn't believe that he has to follow any rules. Yours and dad's rules in your own home mean nothing to him or his friends. That he can play his drums as loud as he wants. If he wants to stay out all night he does. I know mom, you lost control." There was silence. That silence haunts me today.

See Phillip had his driver's license and he was to drive me to my medical appointments so as our dad didn't lose a day of work. When you immigrate to a country, challenges to forge ahead have many uphill battles. Money is a major asset to providing for your family. I had no choice but to rely on him so my health could be restored. So telling my father wasn't an option. So sitting next to Philip in a hospital waiting room morphed my spirit. I stared at the kids with cancer and felt their pain. Mine just wasn't visible. The deeper pain came when I gained the courage to tell my mother what her son had done. Her expression was blank. What seemed like hours were just minutes when she collected her thoughts and said avoiding eye contact, "you're not going to say anything to anyone are you"? Every time I see a Saint Bernard I get goose bumps. I ironically chose her to be The Sheep Dog.

CHAPTER FOUR

Counselling

In Catherine's office I always felt safe. There was an inviting feeling really. Sometimes I'd get a bit uncomfortable when I could smell fresh bread cooking in the kitchen. They had an inspected kitchen in the building for The Meals on Wheels program. Such a wonderful program really, helping the recluse. Often I wondered if the familiar faces in the reception area waiting for counselling were mocked by clues of their past? Never an empty seat in the lobby, that's for sure. Not sure how many were Catholic?

Catherine had such a sweet demeanour. Lady-like in how she would sit. I loved how she learned to be okay in her own body. She'd sometimes wear a sweater because the air conditioning was too high, just draped over her shoulders. She looked as though she armed herself in the event she needed it. This is why I needed her. I had not been prepared.

"So", she began "the wink, let's start there." Oh my, my heart beat with intensity. She knew how to get to a core emotion that's for sure. My body started to feel the rush in temperature, my hands sweating. Wow, was all I could think of. That combined with the smell of yeast, I rocked.

"Ninety second rule, ninety second rule" Catherine stated. I heard it and needed it to register as I sat. It did. This was a code to myself to allow ninety seconds to go by before you respond. Studies show that the first ninety seconds is the reactionary time frame. Deep breaths and focus thought of a safe place are highly recommended. I went to my internal garden that I had been tending to. It was looking more vibrant with each session.

"Yes" I said feeling ready to move forward in our discussion. See after I found that Carmen had his hand in our mother' bank account, Nick and I brought it to Phillip's attention. His reaction was surprising. See Nick and I were not fan's of Phillip for sometime. Phillip and Nick hadn't talked for twenty years. Stood side by side at our father's funeral and didn't speak one word. But Nick convinced me that since this pertained to our mother; we needed to unite as a family. We needed to sort through together to get an explanation behind her money going to gambling. After all, our father left our mother money for her retirement, and who knows how long a person will live? Diane had met Nick during this time. She must have loved him because she stuck around.

So a meeting was set up at our mother's. Our mother was even present. She seemed excited that we were all visiting at the same time. She even got our names wrong. This hadn't happened for twenty years. Perhaps the unusual attendance of all together was the issue? She put coffee on. Carmen was not in attendance though. There was a high roller event at the Casino. So with all the copies of bank accounts and bank transactions laid out on the flimsy kitchen tablecloth, the information screamed out for itself. Pension cheques not fully deposited. Retirement funds transferred to a personal bank account. Withdrawal slips with signatures that were not our mothers. This signature was in traditional black printing on white paper staring us all in the face, Carmen.

Something was askew especially since our mother had forgotten how to make coffee? Response from Philip was shocking really. He nodded and nodded. This left him speechless for a bit. As he tried to gather his thoughts, I tried to align the tablecloth. It had one of those inexpensive flimsy padding that just moved more often then it should.

Finally, after watching him put a pair of glasses on the tip of his nose to scan the bank documents as though he was a chartered accountant, I regretted thinking he had an opinion. He worked as a janitor. But to his credit he nodded with some sort of sincerity, cleared his throat and said "I will talk to Carmen about this and get an explanation and get back to you guys and lets put all this family stuff behind us and move forward."

Paul, myself, Nick and Diane walked out of our mother's home stunned that this was all it would take to patch up family confusion. A war, if you will. Mending a tapestry of possibilities to form a new cloth seemed exciting. Years that had been unfortunately behind us and full grown children in the spot of toddlers now, was inviting. All the years to catch up with the children's lives such as weddings and grand kids, left us with a sensation that hope was in the air.

Weeks passed and I received a phone call from Nick. "Have you heard from Philip", I hadn't. I nodded while on the phone waiting for a response before I figured out he hadn't seen me say no. "No" I stated, "not one call or a missed call." "What do you think we should do?" Nick questioned. I didn't want to have any dealings with him and because Nick was the one who posed the original idea that we needed to work as a family, I said "You should call him." As apprehensive as he was, we did feel that the last visit went well and perhaps Philip had just been busy. A half hour later I received a call with more swearing than I care to share. Suddenly Nick was accused of wanting our mother's money, not only her money but her house? I was shocked. Wasn't sure if Nick had misused his prescribed medication, after all we had brought this information to Philip? "What"? "What are talking about?" I said half laughing thinking I had not heard correctly. "Yah, you heard right and he is accusing you and Paul of the same thing!" Being in disbelief I shook my head thinking, what the hell was going on! "Oh" he continued, "and he put his name on mom's bank account as a joint owner!"

With no other options as it wasn't working at the family level, I called the barrister's office that held my mother's legal documents. He was taken back by what I had told him and the misuse of our mother's estate. He vehemently stated to me "you walk your mother into her bank and cease that bank account. You are a Power of Attorney and so named are being held responsible for the misuse"!

I was shocked. I had not received my copy of any P.O.A. document. So being a compliant soul and afraid of any financial repercussions, I did just that. A new bank account was secured. Nick and I were pleased at the quick direction and the safety now of our mother's finances and sad to think this possibility of reunion would never take place now. Out of courtesy I wrote a letter to each of my bother's explaining the direction I had taken. I was so thoughtful to even include some of the banking transactions that looked criminal in nature.

One visit to my mother's to pick up a gift that we had shared in for the cost of a family member's bridal shower, had me blocked at the entrance way. Philip in his traditional fashion had his shoulder's back; chest puffed not allowing me in. Paul was with me as I feared going alone. My mother who was steps away was crying accusing me of abandoning her. She was coached, no doubt. I had been the only one taking her to doctor appointments and shopping for years. Paul and I looked at each other in disbelief, wondering what the hell was going on. Finally, Carmen who was home this time walked out on to the porch and sat, his face red. Paul talking to him about the misuse of funds, all the while Philip is pushing me out the door, winking at me with his left eye. I am trying to push the door forward while he is pushing it against me, all the while continuing to wink. Unsure if there is a problem with his eye, I kept looking at it until it finally made sense. He was mocking me about what he had done to me when I was fifteen years old. Stunned and not allowing ninety seconds, I raised my right index finger and said "You will never get on top of me again"! As he continued to wink at me, he got close, just as his wife and daughter who were in the home, jumped out of no where as they were hiding in the house and screamed out "that's not the real story, that's not the real story"! He whispered softly so no one else could hear, "sometimes good people do evil things", and slammed the door in my face.

My sister in law Diane was just told of that incident months ago and encouraged me to learn to stand up for myself. It was nice to have a female family member for support. She was the one in fact that told me "if you ever get a chance, you look him in the eye and tell him you will never get on top of me again".

"So" Catherine stated, "anything to share"? Well, in fact there was. After the rage subsided, beyond ninety seconds I felt I could talk. I heard "Katia.....Katia are you okay?"

I became present and said, "Wow that moment just cut real deep."

"How so" said Catherine. "Well" I started, "see part of me wanted to believe that that moment so long ago was just a stupid teenage mistake. A jock that was full of himself. But what cuts so deep, is when he winked, he was mocking me. He remembers everything and was proud of it."

At that moment I watched Catherine's face looking for a response from me. I was numb. I felt re victimized. Even though the session was only an hour, I felt like thirty of it was in shock. I could see that Rottweiler chained in that junk yard with foam of saliva dripping and a sheep dog in the distance. See I had depicted myself as a spirited puppy. It was Catherine's facial expression that had me questioning myself.

Then I realized that that was not a dog it was a stage of a dog's growth. I was startled. I stumbled trying desperately to over correct my response. I realize at that moment how much of an easy prey I was.

CHAPTER FIVE

Leaving the Cemetery

We had just narrowed out of the iron gates of St. Anthony's graveyard. I was mentally visualizing Steve's aunt being pushed in that cemetery plot. I started laughing to myself. Paul looked into his rear view mirror and saw me. "What's so funny?" I stared back directly into the mirror and said "thank you".

"For what" asked Paul?

"For being you", I responded. Paul was not raised in Evandale.

They call people who move into town imports and the locals never really accept them. They can put on a decent smile, but for the most part they really don't want to hear what they have to say. They feel threatened, as though their customs or routines could be challenged? That the bedroom community that they support could one day turn into a Metropolis. Soon there will be drugs and crime in their community and a large presence of other races. Soon the face of the community would be mixed with different points of view, different ideas. Fear was the common approach on how life was lived here. Sadly though, drugs were already here. People just chose to ignore. Makes them feel better.

Carmen had a knack of keeping unfamiliar faces at a distance. He'd be pleasant, don't get me wrong. To your face he was funny and informative. He loved to read. A decent education as well, just not completed. The more he read, the more complicated his thoughts seemed. He learned it was best to keep unfamiliar faces at a distance. Our dad always had concerns. Carmen's repetitiveness seemed peculiar. He drove only the same streets and if a road was closed he panicked. Seemed strange because the size of the town was maybe a radius of twenty miles wide and the familiarity of the community wasn't difficult to learn. He only lived in this town and was afraid to leave it. Loved the outskirts of town where the Race track was though. In fact best to not talk about that at all. Our father had concerns about the late night card games and the lack of funds to support the habit. Our mother defended him. He was her first born.

Theresa was the third born and a girl. Her duties within her childhood home as a young girl was to cook and clean. Learn to sew which became a skill she could rely on. She needed to when her parents urged her to leave because the war had depleted funds and food was scarce. A young woman and her siblings became a burden. They were instructed to leave and carve out a life of their own. One way tickets were bought so they can begin a new life in Canada. A family member agreed to sponsor them and would try to help. Rumours in Italy were the streets in Canada were lined with gold. Stories of a new beginning, was exciting for our grandmother. See she wanted desperately to immigrate also, so by pushing her kids, then it would make it easier for her. This selfish streak wasn't a trait that Theresa liked about her mother. That's when she decided she would be a supportive parent if God granted her children, no matter what.

Theresa struggled to speak up before immigrating. She liked a young man in their neighbourhood. But she was too scared to say anything. She thought talking to a priest might be the route to go. Father Bernardin knew she had a troubled heart that one day she stayed after Sunday mass. But young Theresa was burdened with guilt. She walked away from him and turned at a distance. Just staring as he walked away. You are not supposed to defy the family.

A young Christian girl was supposed to respect authority. And that she did. She arrived on a ship that set sail for fifteen days across the Atlantic with a cousin, both teenagers, and scared. Uncertain on what lied beyond the water. So when she met Rocco and decided Life had little options, and married, her first child was her reason to forge ahead. Someone needed her. He knew she loved him, that's why the deception was so easy.

When Paul first came into the family with his two boys Carmen and Paul enjoyed conversations on music. Both loved the Beatles. Both played football in high school and loved trivia. The boys looked up to him and thought it cool that he had a head full of information. He talked in length about the mysteries of Oak Island or the Bermuda triangle. How the Mayan civilization just vanished and there was no visible exodus out. Theory was they went up. How intriguing he could be. His story telling abilities were intriguing at best. I developed so many interests because of the ability to transcend the barriers of a small community because of the interest that was planted into my brain at such a young age. He inspired me to read, and because of this I trusted him implicitly. After all he brought an expansive world to me.

What he didn't realize that later in life I learned that Story telling is just that. See this Story telling became so elaborate that our mother refused to be buried next to her husband. Carmen told her how our father and Paul had stolen her money. How our dad gambled the family's money and was an alcoholic. Our father was unbeknownst to us a villain created out of desperation because when you are too embarrassed to admit that your life was a failure, best to blame someone else. And actually a dead person makes it easier.

See, Carmen was the first person I told about what Philip had done because Philip had bullied him. Called him names, and refused to be associated with him. For years Carmen was tormented by Philip and it pained him. This is why I felt it was easy to tell him first. He felt the pain of a kid brother. Bullied and demeaned. I understood his struggles. It would be wonderful to be able to discuss the pain with someone and deal with it with someone who could relate. But Carmen did nothing. He was worse than my mother. He said nothing. After a long silence he got off his lawn chair and went in the house to make a sandwich. In counselling I had depicted him as a lazy bloodhound.

So how was it possible that Philip was accusing Nick and I of wanting our mother's money, or her house? Completing ignoring the paper trail? This just seemed odd. How could evidence be dismissed? I had to follow the invisible chain backward. Once I saw the tapestry that was weaved I knew I no longer was a puppy and had nothing to fear. See Paul had been divorced and had learned how to manoeuvre in a court room. He borrowed The Rules of Civil Procedure and represented himself. He did better than the two previous lawyers he had hired. So by daring to forge ahead I had nothing to lose. This was a new tapestry for me. See my past had crippled me. My future was empowering me.

CHAPTER SIX

Counselling

Catherine had been fighting a cold, so the tissue held dual purposes today. Dressed in a white pinstripe, navy dress which truly suited her, I could not sit before complimenting her. I sat with ease as she situated herself looking forward to the next hour. Each session built on the previous. I was learning to actually hear what I was saying. Also learning that I had not the skills before coming here, at least not visible to me. But it was becoming more evident each time. "I brought something here for you to look at" I stated, offering a self created bound book of bank withdrawals and transfers all with Carmen's signature. Catherine secured it and lowering her reading glasses from the top of her head flipped through the pages diligently. Her face perused with a gentle up and down while turning. When she got to the last page she was silent. Never saw this blank, pale look before. The hesitation, then a gentle nod generated with a seemingly understanding. She placed the glasses back on top of her head and looked me straight in the eye. I knew she understood.

"So" Catherine started, "I must compliment you on your ability to put all this factual information together like this. Perhaps being a writer is a calling for you".

I smiled feeling complimented and hopeful that perhaps someday facts could be read by the proper authority.

"So" she stated "it seems so straight forward. Dates, amounts, bank accounts the details tell the story. Your letters, lawyers responses, cross examinations, court proceedings. Each identified sections is like a section of a quilt, when you stitch the entirety of the pages the story is right there."

I nodded with satisfaction that my puppy like demeanour had not given up. She laid the book on the end of her lap and leaned towards me. "I want to share something with you that I learned while I was in the Social Work program. In behavioural psychology Pavlov's dog had learned to salivate each time he heard the bell ring. A neutral person would introduce food and the dog immediately salivated. Then they introduced a bell. Each time this person repeated the experiment they got the same response. Then they introduced just the bell and the dog salivated. No meat, just a bell. When they introduced a different person to conduct the experiment they would get the same response. This was determined to be a conditioned response. So, because of this he had retrained his brain. It was a simple but all the same interesting study." I knew of this study but didn't quite understand how this study was relative to my issues. She watched how I was processing the information.

Slowly she started, "Another story about the elephant with the rope," She stated. Where a grandfather brings his grandchild to a circus and the grandson sees that a large elephant has a rope around its right ankle. That's it, just a thin rope. The young boy looking confused tilting his head while trying to understand how such a massive animal was constrained by it, turned to his grandfather and asked, "How isn't he running away?"

His grandfather was impressed on his grandson's observations and responded, "See, when that big elephant was just a baby elephant he had large chains secured around his ankle. Each time he would try to escape the chains would tear into his flesh causing great pain. So over time the baby elephant had become conditioned to its own prison. The trainers know that the elephant could easily run away with just that thin rope but it chooses not to. The grandson looked overwhelmed at the explanation because the largest animal on our planet had restricted its own freedom.

I sat absorbing the information and in time started nodding. Catherine watched, hopeful at the response. "My, those are very interesting", I stated. I stared at the abstract art on the wall in front of me. It seemed odd how time can feel like it doesn't exist when knowingness captures you. Catherine gave me my booklet back and asked "Is there anything you want to discuss?"

After what seemed like hours, I sat up, placed the booklet against my chest, hugging it. The words, the facts, were more comforting to me now. I was now armed with the insight and fortitude to emotionally forge forward.

CHAPTER SEVEN

On our way to The Grotto

We took the back roads to the Grotto. Deliberately broke the line of the procession as we knew a short cut. Diane was crying in the backseat so I hugged her. She missed Nick. The day was bringing back far too many memories. Kyle grabbed some gum out of the glove compartment and offered everyone some. I wasn't convinced it was edible as it had sat there for at least six months. He chose a piece. His jaw looked like it was really working but I knew the growling sound at the gravesite meant someone skipped breakfast.

To console Diane I offered her a tissue from a bunch I had taken at the funeral home, followed by a bigger hug. Then I looked her right into her green eyes and raised my cross and said" do you want this?" She began to snicker. Wasn't sure if she really did or not. We just left the subject.

The autumn leaves were starting to fall. The crispness of there vibrant foliage was beautiful, calming. We passed homes that had yards filled with them disguising that a lawn really existed. Kids were outside playing in them while some were raking them with adult supervision. The ride to the Grotto was pleasant, quiet but pleasant.

I was beginning to rake in my own internal garden. Ridding myself of what no longer served its purpose. I looked at the clay crucifix and could see a painful image. I could see in my minds eye, Sister Elizabeth teaching a Religion class, hearing her firmly stating, "He died for your sins".

I thought my sins? Who's exactly? That fixed bronze glaze was simply a statue. It wasn't a person. I thought I was not to worship idols? The internal confusion of beliefs imposed upon me with the progression of First Communion, Confirmation, as ceremonies of advancement and advancement to what really, salvation? Members of the Vatican and The Diocese had basic training in this as well, so why the lawsuits?

I felt a need to release the ethereal rope. I felt the desire to be free from restrictions that had woven a tight aura of being less than what my potential was. I could sense the freedom of spring.

We arrived at the Grotto minutes before the procession line. Paul was searching for a parking spot and he landed one next to a relative who was getting out of his car with his second wife. Not convinced there will not be a third. I could hear Paul say to me "don't do it Katia, don't do it". He could see my blood pressure starting to rise. Philip had chosen a cousin, Luke, to be a pall bearer. Philip overlooked selecting Kyle and Paul. It was a deliberate tactic to appease his ego and a tactic to mock.

"Hey Luke" I piped up after getting out of the vehicle before it came to a complete stop. His wife walking sheepishly off to his right, said "uh, yeah".

Immediately, I confidently said while looking directly in his eyes of which he tried to avoid contact and stated "Who gives you the right to take the place of a grandson"? He appeared uncomfortable, his face pale and said "Philip asked". He avoided contact the remainder of that afternoon. He knew our mother wouldn't have chosen him. But he got a hefty commission for selling her home. Philip and Luke had some similarities that were unappealing.

When I wandered in with my crucifix and family, my stride showed determination. There were more tables than people who attended the service I noticed. I was greeted by a hostess who offered her condolences and gracefully pointed me in a direction of where the family was to sit. I looked at the probability that she didn't know the family war and walked to the other side. I placed my clay statue on the table next to a white rose in a centerpiece. Wine was placed on the tables and I proceeded to tell Paul, while turning, noticing a bartender wiping the counter," How lovely, an open bar".

The people arrived. Aunts, uncles, cousins, second cousins, friends, neighbors and of course Philip's lawyer. A free meal couldn't be overlooked. My heart began beating intensely. I was still waiting to hear from The Law Society to bring his conduct into question. A Catholic, Italian lawyer that should have been named Judas, that is if people still allow that name?

Judas did have another name it was Carlo Scarpenza. He is a short man of five foot five, a snake. Slender build and a voice that was irritating. All too often I noticed he had a slight lisp that Paul and I could detect. If anyone else had, they certainly contained their composure. He had a bald spot that the front comb over didn't quite cover. The light at the right angle would gleam off it. Almost like a ricochet. I had a hard time not laughing to myself. He was very theatrical in the court as he gestured frequently with his hands. His voice projecting with exaggerations and his body language over emphasized with shoulders back. Apparently the judge couldn't see that reflection. She was at a disadvantage sitting higher. She had been so drawn in by the dramatic performance that she ruled based on it. The paperwork that had all the truths was never brought forward. My slender handsome lawyer had missed this in litigation 101.

This ruling had removed me from my position as a Power of Attorney. I had been advised that I could use estate funds as a Power of Attorney to defend my mother's documents; the one's that Philip was trying desperately to gain control over. So desperate actually that he walked our mother into his lawyer's office weeks after we brought thievery to his attention. Monies mishandled by

Carmen. Mr Scarpenza knew that documents were secured by a previous lawyer and could do nothing to interfere with them. But as embellished stories surfaced and Carmen convinced himself that our father had stolen the money and gambled it away leaving our mother destitute, Philip believed him. Odd, as our father had been deceased for decades. He believed him so much that the story morphed itself into a distortion of bullshit. So much bullshit, that soon I was being accused of stealing money even though facts explained the truth. Or so this was the story my lawyer said who was always unprepared before court.

Eventually his lawyer went so far to order a Capacity Assessment on our mother. Philip booked the appointment. Philip paid the bill for the appointment. But Philip claims Theresa wanted documents changed? Interestingly enough, she failed the assessment. I thought this legal issue was done. But when I depicted Philip as a rottweiler I knew he was just that, hungry for power.

What was the truth behind this need to gain control? Especially since thievery was brought to his attention? Carmen had been feeding a gambling addiction by withdrawing these funds. Nick, Diane Paul and I had brought this to his attention at our mother's house. Nick had made the decision to solve this issue at the family level even though we were anything but a family. Philip actually showed concern. Dramatically of course, like his lawyer. The two had been well matched. I would have to describe Mr. Scarpenza as a Jack Russell, annoying, busy and always on the hunt.

When Philip finally got back to Nick after discussing the issue with Carmen, only to accuse Nick of stealing our mother's money, and wanting her home. This was an odd reaction because bank documents tell the story beautifully. Odd because Carmen had lied to the police about the time frame I told him about the abuse. Odd that Philip could have sought Carmen's removal as a co-attorney, but was suing me for my position? Odd really how this happened just after the secret got out.

Shortly after I was served documents, an Application for Guardianship Title was being sought. I secured a lawyer. His lawyer argued in court that he was trying to protect Theresa's finances from me. That's why the lawsuit was filed. Odd, because when She was deemed incompetent, our mothers documents stayed as is. Nothing could be changed now. These documents were secure. That is until a crafty lawyer finds a way to get to them. Apparently legally isn't always how the game is played. Philip showed him a chequebook. A bell must have chimed. I was acting as my mother in a P.O.A. capacity.

I was told by my lawyer, that when I show that all the financials were in order that this lawsuit would go away. What I have learned through court battles is that who so ever can drag out the suit longest benefits the most. Lawyers I mean. A strategy that has crippled the very nature of what the law should be. Motion after motion I watched and felt the integrity of truth become so distorted that the distortion became the revised truth. So much so that the evidence became more burdensome to reveal than to dramatically stage a performance. I wouldn't even go as far to say an Academy award performance. I am more inclined to say a kindergarten Christmas play. After all, my brother's lawyer is only five foot five.

While the guests were sitting and grouping themselves with those they chose to sit with, I caught Philip and his family entering. Philip's son, who was six foot two, with a balding head and tattoos all over his body and piercing in his eyebrows and lip looked straight at me trying to stare me down. I felt inclined to raise the crucifix but I decided to just laugh. Laugh so much that his billboard body was a display of the same crippling weakness he and his father shared. If Satan had chosen a companion, he was here today having lunch.

The food was as usual, an excellent meal cooked by the elderly women of the community who perfected it. Our neighbour that was sitting by Diane had noticed the stare down by Philip junior and laughed while buttering his roll. "Oh to be thirty and stupid again" he said.

Kyle got up to visit with a cousin at the table next to us. Chatter filled the room. People walked and visited over the passing hours and my mother's memory was tossed around. There were stories of childhood and how she endured the Second World War. Stories of how she and our father met. Everyone had a story. Sadly though, the story of how an incapable woman had lost her mind was out manoeuvred by her son and a lawyer. That's the story she didn't deserve. Especially since the law states that "Justice is not only to be done, it is to be seen to be done"

I took a metaphorical step back and zoomed in. Watching the visitors and seeing those autumn leaves fall in my mind and knowing I have the ability to rake it all up. Self Representation can be a daunting task, but so be it an empowering one. I was no longer a puppy which I had identified with. By daring to challenge the situation, my spirit directed me forward. Any chains that had restrained me were purposefully removed. I collected all the qualities I knew I had and forged ahead.

CHAPTER EIGHT

Leaving The Grotto

The cars were leaving the Grotto and I made sure I wasn't going to be remaining with my brothers and his family. I said my goodbyes to distant relatives and friends. Raised my crucifix and gathered the white rose. The thorn had dug into my thumb on my right hand and slowly a trickle of blood was noticeable. Diane offered me one of her tissues to wipe it. I thought about how Sister Elizabeth would talk about the blood of Christ and how he was crucified by Pontius Pilate. How she told us that he washed his hands to rid himself of the act of doing so. Was he a man with a conscious perhaps?

Mr. Scarpenza walked past me and began a gesture to offer his condolences. Paul, Kyle Diane and I were dumbfounded by his extended hand and before the others spoke up, I said "I don't think so"! We turned our heads as he continued to walk toward his car. Kyle immediately leaned into me and whispered "karma's a bitch". I looked at my crucifix and wasn't sure about the Catholic Law regarding the trendy statement and stated, "Law Society should be making there decision soon".

As we were shuffling ourselves into the car I refused to look back at my brothers who were carting out all the left over food. Odd how Philip was writing a cheque when he wasn't even named Executor.

Carmen had arbitrarily given him his position. Little thought about a legal requirement was even entertained. The funeral home director had noted that my mother's jewellery had been handed to Philip, the Executor. I didn't have the time to explain to him that he had committed fraud.

With the tissue wrapped around my thumb, I traded places with Diane in the backseat. Paul and Kyle resumed their places. I placed the white rose on the back deck, laying it by the back window. I knew the sun wouldn't prolong its lifespan as its demise was already in the process. I thought the rays of the sunlight would capture the beauty that still existed for the time being.

While staring at its soft petals and naturally crafted beauty I was mesmerized at how nature had known to design this. The precision of an intelligent coding that was so deliberate in its mathematics, that artists spend hours trying to duplicate. Thorns so deliberately placed to protect it was so endearing to me. I smiled. I looked at my thumb and the slight cut was nothing more than a rose doing its job, protecting.

Between searching for a radio station and random conversations in the car about the luncheon, I found myself drifting back in time.

I could picture the petals of my mothers life peel away, each year falling ever so delicately. I could visualize her as I created in my thoughts her versions of her childhood. The stucco home situated on an olive orchard with her and her siblings working the land while a father was absent during war. A widowed grandmother who settled there to help take care of the children and whose difficult life was reduced to gratefulness and love of family. While a mother sewed to help bring some money into the household.

The bombardment of shells dropping during night skies and the possibility of personal death was high. Neighbours relied on each other during the destruction that was happening around them. They united with spiritual courage to forge ahead. Hope was a petal everyone held so tightly to. My mother talked extensively about her doll Mary. A dishtowel rolled tightly. She'd share her fears with her and her hopes of a future, privately in a closet in her bedroom where she'd hide during the bomb attacks.

She'd share how her mother would punish her for disobeying chores. At seven she was responsible for making bread for the household. At nine she was sent to a woman to learn how to sew to help make money for the family. Disobedience she was taught was against God's wishes. When her mother found her hiding underneath her bed because she was teaching herself to read, she felt the pain of being spanked. Reading was deemed to be impractical when the answer to their family troubles was money. Even though she loved the stories from her tattered bible, work was priority.

Disobedience was the sin of the time. As she aged and room in the house was confined, there was difficulty sustaining the household needs. With this impending challenge, she and a cousin Dante were told they were to immigrate to Canada. A sponsor had been secured, her uncle of which she never met. With no questions, a time frame was given and it was met. Two oblivious teenagers waved goodbye on a massive ship without stabilizers heading across the Atlantic to Nova Scotia. Days of vomiting and uncertainty plagued them. With one hundred dollars and a suitcase sparse with personal items, their future was beckoning. Fear was at the helm. She had been taught to pray and it was in full force. Pity and anger, along with sadness and abandonment were emotions that were as volatile as the waves.

When the shipped docked fifteen days later, little food had been digested and so many others were experiencing the same difficulties. A stranger in the distance on the main deck had an accordion in his suitcase. He pulled it out and with a natural impulse to cheer himself and the saddened faces, he began singing. There were songs about the old country and songs of missing home. There were songs of saying good-bye. Soon it became evident each passenger had similar emotional experiences with tears and lack of expression. Hope was glue that knitted them into a fabric of desperation and community. Soon good byes would be a new journey.

After they docked and they were carted through the immigration process, keeping close to what became their new community, sadness intensified. The shuffling of feet on the wooden floor and lines created to help control the amount of people being funnelled through. The accordion was silenced. The ability to comprehend questions was minimal and few interpreters were earning their pay.

Once the processing was complete and sincere good byes were had, the crowd diminished. Some were going toward the train, some on boats while others waited for pick up. The need to commit emotionally was dangerous as miles would sever possibilities of reunion. Forward was the quest.

My mother boarded what she described as a train to no where. Fear was churning with each chugging of the train car. Watching the passing of forested terrain and towns whisk by her stare. Dante was quiet. He was the eldest son who lost his mother during the birth of his younger brother. A widower had difficulties nurturing. Mood of the times was its time to leave. At sixteen he was on his own, considered a man now. My mother was nineteen and eligible for marriage. Family was praying for marriage for her. Once settled, a home would beckon a residence for future flocks from the old country. She would be praised as the trailblazer.

Praying and devotion to a God would make all things fine. The tattered bible had reiterated to my mother the stories the priests told at Sunday mass. She carried this in her suitcase. At times it became a place of solace to remind her that she could venture through the difficulties. Christ after all had challenges she couldn't even fathom. His experience of crucifixion was a display of pain instilled for her and that she was taught to have reverence and adoration.

She met a man on the train that she sheepishly talked to. He was handsome and financially settled but an Agnostic. His interest in her was noticeable but the fear of his lack of belief was confusing and scarier than her destination to Evandale. After conversations of Jesus, apostles and parables, Bernard Eickmain understood that Theresa's belief had entrenched her into a future of restrictions. His ability to speak her language had been trumped by the burning bush and the story on the mount.

Bernard looked reluctantly at Theresa when the train stopped. Wanting to kiss her as a watchful cousin looked on. He knew not to. He put on his hat and nodded to her and wished her well. She struggled in her heart for years. The thought of a different life was unfathomable. The belief system she conformed to restricted any unfamiliar practices. It was understood that she was to conduct herself with intent on being a dutiful wife to a Catholic, Italian. Love would be favourable but not completely necessary. After all, thou shall not disobey thy mother or thy father.

I thought it odd that she never shared these stories with any other family member. Perhaps sharing with me made it less restrictive in her soul. Perhaps her natural desire of being a woman with ideas and potential had been reduced to servility and persecution. She met our father through an uncle who sponsored her entry into Canada. My father was employed in his restaurant after immigrating two years earlier. He was from a different region of Italy but a good loyal worker and had qualities of a husband. Love would have to follow.

CHAPTER NINE

Leaving The Grotto

Kyle accidentally passed gas and was laughing before the smell had invaded the car completely. "Whoa. My dear god"....laughing and waving my right hand. The tissue fell off. The blood dried. Diane snorted while laughing waving both her hands. That sparked more laughter in the car. I checked to see if the rose had been damaged with the fumes, but fortunately its beauty was still evident.

"Look" Kyle said, pointing left, to the side of the moving car. Philip was passing our car. His family, a girlfriend of Philip jr. and Carmen squeezed into a compact car. "Talk about not following the rules of the road. Look how fast he's driving"? As they passed us I felt inclined to raise my hand and give the finger. I hesitated and raised my crucifix instead. Diane couldn't contain the laughter. Between the smell of gas and now this episode her cheeks were beginning to become sore. "Once an asshole, always an asshole" Kyle said. In unison we all agreed.

We could see some black smoke coming out of Philips tail pipe and knew all to well his vehicle was in some distress. As the drift of grey smoke hovered and slowly dissipated we engaged in conversation about my father. Kyle turned and looked at me and asked "What was Grandpa like?"

Kyle had never met him and had only heard stories. Carmen had on several occasions told him that he had gambled and was a drunk. Kyle being at a disadvantage knew no different. He had heard interesting stories from me. So where was the truth? Why would a grown adult lie? Who benefits from this lie?

Kyle learned in time that grown adults lie for many reasons. They have an ego to protect. After all a wounded ego makes for a severe identity crisis. Even a thorn has a task to protect its flower.

See Carmen had always had high aspirations. Between Conspiracy theories and his interest in Criminal Law, his mind worked overtime. Often times drawing out possible conclusions while his mind raced at an impossible speed. A myriad of possible outcomes entertained him exhausting his ability to focus on a goal. His intrigue with learning how to dodge conclusions and redirecting was skilful. It consumed him really. Never married, never dated, nor finished his schooling. He coined the phrase "art of the twist". An art it was. Perhaps a course should be created and taught. Could be titled "How to destroy the Soul" 101. Would imagine it could fall between the philosophy or theology department? To fall into the Psychology department seems more sinister?

Kyle spoke up and said "so let me get this straight, grandpa didn't drink?"

"No" I laughed, "he drank, and he loved spending time with his friends a few nights a week. They would drink and play cards at the Grotto."

"Grandma said she didn't like it'! Kyle responded.

I explained, "she never really minded, gave her time to watch Wheel of Fortune on TV. She adored Vanna."

Then Kyle stated "So why make it look like he was a drunk if he was just hanging out with friends?"

"Well I stated, it's easy to explain that, because a dead man can't defend himself".

"True" Kyle said.

I responded "See anything can be put into a conversation and when a person isn't there to counter what you're saying, they are at an advantage."

Kyle responded, "but why didn't grandma stop him from making her husband look like a terrible person?"

"Good question I stated, see grandma had chains.

"Chains" Kyle stated.... "what do you mean by that"?

"See Kyle a parent's responsibility is to oversee the growth of their children but not to direct the outcome, best to say, guide them with their own decisions."

"Okay" Kyle uttered. "I get that. "But how did these chains influence Uncle Carmen?

"Well", I started, "if I was afraid of snakes and all the while I was raising you I told you how much I hated and was scared of snakes, the probability is you would be afraid of snakes. I wouldn't have encouraged you to like them; in fact I would do the opposite. Now let's say dad also hated snakes and he reinforced the idea of how scary snakes are and how dangerous they could be, chances are you would be more inclined to not like them."

"Okay" Kyle answered "I get that. But the idea of being chained seems odd".

But if we talked about not liking something when you have no reason to not understand why you don't like something than you have been restricted by conditioning to have my response, not your own response.

"Okay, Kyle uttered. But I still have a brain of my own".

"Yes, of course you do." I stated, laughing. "But if you have never been taught to think for yourself who is at fault? Am I responsible or are you because you admittedly stated you have a brain?"

The mood in the car became quiet. Bridge over Troubled Water had come on the radio. Three out of four of us loved the song.

We shushed Kyle and he got the clue. After the song was done the announcer was asking for the seventh caller to call in to the show to win tickets to The Shrine circus. I turned to Diane and said, "I love the circus" jokingly, "always wanted an elephant." Diane spoke up and said "where on earth would you keep an elephant?" laughing.

Diane had not had counselling so she thought literally.

Paul was involved in raising funds for the organization in the past. Fellow Free Masons gave willingly of their time to do good deeds.

I sat looking at the dried blood on my finger and spit on it, wiping it with the other hand. "One hand washes the other", I said. No different than Carmen and Phillip.

Diane looked at me perplexed.

Kyle said "I am going to dial the number", quickly he used his cell phone. We could hear the busy signal each time. He kept hitting redial and it was on speaker. "Look" I said to Diane, "gone, all gone. Just a small prick left". I showed her my thumb. The crucifix had been sliding off my lap so I readjusted it. I looked into the eyes of the statue and I could still hear the lyrics that had played on the radio. The announcer on the radio mentioned the winner. So Kyle hung up.

While on our way home, I was thinking of all the house chores I needed to tend to. The house had been less of a priority the last few days. If relatives dropped by, a judgement call would certainly be passed. No doubt.

"Too bad you weren't the winner" Diane said to Kyle.

"Yeah" he responded.

"So back to these chains" Kyle turned to look to me. "Are you saying that I am responsible? What about my environment? If I grow up in a household that talks completely negatively about snakes then you have created my ideas?"

"Did I?" I stated.

Kyle pondered and said, "Well think about this, I rely on you and dad to guide me. I am like a blank slate coming into this world. Because you are in a role of trust and I would never think that you are lying to me. So ultimately you would have taught me wrong, but for me I would have thought I was right?"

I interrupted and said "okay, but you said you had a brain so having said that, you're in control of your brain. I can suggest, (I pointed to his phone) technology gives you ample source of information."

"True" Kyle responded.

"So" I explained, "when I die am I still influencing you?"

"Hmm" Kyle said. "I guess not, because you would be a memory."

"So," I questioned "if I am just a memory, who owns the idea?"

Thinking, he quietly uttered "I guess me".

I asked respectively "Who controls you?" while fixing the crucifix and reaching for the rose.

CHAPTER TEN

Drive Home

We had redirected our journey home by going through the industrial part of town. It's on the east side of Evandale, just outside the area where the Grotto was. We lived on the Westside. By cutting through the quarry we would get home ten minutes earlier. Unfortunately the train that was heading into the area had been moving quicker than expected. The lights began flashing as the bars lowered just as we were nearing it. If we had left minutes before, we could have avoided this distraction.

"Almost" Paul said as he pressed the brakes. The flashing red lights and the repetitive dinging kept us limited behind the barrier. All of us looked out the window, to our left to see how long the train was. We were looking for the engine. It wasn't in sight.

With the dinging sound I found myself thinking of Catherine's session when she talked about Pavlov and his dog. How the experiment had broken a barrier of its own regarding conditioning. I found myself smiling. The dog had been trained to salivate. So what would it take to reverse this training I thought, days or years?

Kyle asked Paul "Do you think we will be home before four o'clock?" Paul looked at his watch and laughed. "It's three, so we better be. We only live fifteen minutes away. We all laughed. Someone was getting bored.

Kyle asked "Who inherited grandpa's accordion"?

"How did you know he played one? I asked.

Kyle responded, "When I was really small grandma would sing in Italian to a cassette tape that he recorded."

I got chills. I had taped him. My father was self taught, learned by ear. He loved to play. His right foot always had a tapping action when he was enthralled in his song.

"The whooshing of the train made a sound like that cassette. It wasn't the best quality", Kyle mentioned.

Surprisingly I had come to find out that moment from Kyle, that he had listened frequently to it and loved looking at old photos with his grandma. Paul and I didn't know. Apparently Kyle knew something was wrong with her memory. She shared that she was loosing things all the time; she even tried to answer the remote control for the television when the telephone was ringing. But other times, she was perfect. She even mentioned to him that Philip would pick Carmen up and drive to the Casino together. She talked extensively about their wins and losses. How sad, she felt for both. Often they attended the free entertainment. My understanding is free entertainment carries a large hidden price tag. He even thought it odd the day someone showed up at the door looking for Carmen because he was selling a female watch he had posted on an internet sight. How fortunate he was to have these memories of his grandma. No one could steal that from him.

Music was an important part of Theresa's life. Now her memories will melodically enchant each of us in our own way. I was looking forward to the response from The Law Society. Conflict of Interest determination would be music to my ears. A judge that had made decisions on false information would be a tune the public would love to hear. A tune I will make certain gets played, over and over to scare the snakes away.

"Grandma donated that accordion. She knew it would just sit on a shelf after he died. She wanted it to bring enjoyment to others. It was meant to be used, not gather dust." I stated. An accordion to

Theresa brought hope. The man that had sung so long ago on the ship she sailed on to come to Canada had forged this strength. He lived in that moment and didn't succumb to worry. Forging with spirit and determination would be the best way to carve out an uncertain future.

I found myself missing my father, a man of great value. Religion was not an important priority to him. Keeping your moral compass was. Though raised Catholic, work had allowed for his escape early on in life. Animals needed tending to and he'd laugh and say, "God wasn't showing up to milk them".

Practicality should have been his middle name. When you have experienced poverty, value becomes an essential perspective. Old shoes are not thrown out. Furniture gets rebuilt. Food is grown. So when a lawyer slithers his way into a opportune moment to blindly squeeze the belongings of an uneducated man and his spouse, whom worked hard for what they owned, one gathers their crucifix, stands up and learns the rules of law.

As the train passed and the dinging subsided, the passage way was now free for movement. We made it home, crucifix in hand.

CHAPTER ELEVEN

Home

The dog had not been let out the entire time we were away. So Paul unlocked the door and without any ability to control her direction Quasar bolted past him directly to the back yard. After finishing up what she needed to, she quickly darted for a head scratch and a belly rub. She is a golden retriever that was a delight to have. Always playful with anyone who came to the door or visited. I raised my cross to show her, and she had no reaction. She bolted to Diane. How she loved her. The treats in her coat pocket didn't hurt.

Quasar was a soul of complete love really, except for one male mailman. She disliked him. This particular mailman was a relief worker and appeared to only fill in when other workers were on vacation or sick. So we would only see him periodically at best. He appeared to be a friendly man, but somehow Quasar instinctively would growl and jump, ready to attack. Feeling sorry for him, as he loved dogs and owned one as well, he tried to ease into a welcome with her, sometimes even bringing biscuits. Bribery works for people so why not animals? Quasar was different. She couldn't be bought.

After being home for a few hours, unwinding and getting things in order. I placed the crucifix on the dining room table. Our dining room table was no last supper; it was just a dusty wood table that could only sit eight. I put the rose in a small vase of water. This new bronze addition didn't seem to coordinate with our decor.

We had decorated with lots of bright colors and the sadness of the figure would draw down the vibrancy of the hues. The heaviness of the cross appeared burdensome, with a sense of restriction. A man nailed because history tells us a story and conflicting stories at that. There are countless bibles on shelves in homes that speak of stories. Pagans tell their tale. Christians tell their tale. Muslims tell their tale. Hindu's tell their tale, while Mythology tells their tales. All stories, that reduce themselves to the telephone game through out time. Generations passing on a message that gets distorted and then worshiped. Seems generations have behaved like children at an infancy stage of intelligence with divisions of power and abuse of it as well. Restrictive nails that bind because of fear of being immoral. All the while those who are so convincing hire lawyers and conceal secrets.

We could hear this slow, fierce growl from the entrance way. Quasar had lowered her body. Her back end raised and her front paws ready. She looked like a marathon runner ready for the whistle. Not knowing what her issue was, soon we heard the lid of the mailbox close. The neighbours' dog started to bark as the mailman was heading across the driveway to his home. The barks were unfortunately not in unison and the noise became bothersome.

Quasar raised her body, scratching the inside of the screen door. When I went to secure her from breaking open the door, I got sight of the mailman. It was Simon, the one she hated. At a distance, he and I made eye contact and he just shrugged his shoulders and shook his head. Felt sorry for him. As for Quasar, she was glad he was gone. The panting afterwards needed some words of comforting to settle her. "Mailman's gone now, its okay."

Paul yelled up from the family room and said "it's all good; she's trying to keep those bills from coming to the house." I laughed. Thought perhaps we should keep Quasar outside, couldn't hurt? But her sweet demeanour for the rest of us would be the toss. Inside she stays I thought over patting her head.

I stepped out. Retrieved the mail and today there was a whole slew of envelopes secured with a blue elastic. Sometimes that was the best thing you got with mail delivery. As Quasar was following me back in, sniffing at the items, I wandered to the dining room table and one by one read who the sender was. I dropped the envelopes in piles as to who they belonged to. Kyle had a pile. Bills had a pile. Paul had a pile.

Kyle got the first two. One his vehicle was being recalled. Another credit card approval and a few coupons for half off pizza orders that pretty well belong to anyone who claimed it, as well as a hydro bill and a letter from the law society. I froze. I found myself staring at the envelope with Private and Confidential stamped on it.

Paul called up from his desk and without turning asked, "Anything of importance?" I didn't know how to respond. Quasar stood loyal by my side as I was at a loss for words. The excitement of a positive determination that the lawyer had conducted himself improperly was the message my heart was sending to my brain. On the other hand my brain was sending my heart a message, saying they found no issue with his conduct. What to do. What to do. Fear had immobilized me. I could see the crucifix and raised it so as it could see the letter. There was no response.

"Anything" Paul asked?

"Actually, there is" I said humbly. Besides pizza being half price, I have a response from The Law Society."

Paul immediately ran up the stairs. Quasar got excited, thinking its time to play. Paul tried to settle her and I said, while gently raising it to the light to see through the envelope, "do you want to open it?"

Paul gently grabbed it from my hand and we both took a breath. With delicateness about his tear, as I watched, fear consumed me.

Diane walked into the room with Kyle. They had been in the living room watching television. "What's going on?" Kyle asked.

To distract him from the importance of this letter opening ritual, I lifted his two articles of mail and said, "These are for you".

He looked at them but did nothing. Diane noticed the Sender's address and the Confidential print and suspected that this is what we were waiting for.

"Oh my, she said, is that what I think it might be?" I looked at her and nodded.

Paul opened the letter and it appeared lengthy. A few pages stapled. As his eyes streamed back and forth over the pages and the first page moved to the back. His face seemed serious and unable to discern. Kyle and I shrugged shoulders not sure want to make of it.

"Time to get on with our life" Paul said.

Unsure what that even meant. Diane said "bad news?"

He hesitated and he said "it all depends on how you interpret it?"

"How so" I said. My life had been in a state of turmoil for five years and making light of this now was not what I could emotionally handle.

Paul piped up and said "perhaps Quasar is far more intelligent then we ever knew?"

I had always thought she was intelligent for a dog. As a dog owner I felt I needed to be loyal to her as she was to me. So I responded jokingly, "Well of course". I stroked her fur and got a hand full of it. "Probably a reason she doesn't like Simon. Maybe she senses the sadness he has brought to this household?"

"There has been acknowledgement from The Law Society" Paul said with a big grin. Raised the letter high up and said, "not giving up has paid off"!

Quasar must have felt the rise of energy in the room because she started to jump, her front claws on Paul's sweater. It all seemed surreal. There were conversations happening around me, but my mental state was on mute. I could only hear my heart beat and it was intense. I thought of the journey that had impacted me and my family. I could see and hear the judge in Division Court granting me permission to appeal to the Appeal Court. When I was granted the Motion to move forward by that judge I felt hopeful, only to be robbed by the three judges who could not interfere in the lower' court decision. I had been imprisoned, nailed to a circumstance by the hands of others. With the truth of professional misconduct being casually overlooked, I forged on. Today was the day. Determination was paying off. Rules of the Court had been breached.

I picked up the letter after the commotion had settled. A tribunal would be responsible to make sure the public was not in harm's way. My mother now qualified as public.

How proud of myself and Paul's encouragement. I lifted Quasar's front legs and danced with her, her large body bumping the dining room table and shaking the crucifix causing it to slide. A tear fell, then another. I can bring forward a lawsuit later, god willing? I hoped for so long that tales would fall and the truth be seen. Would they?

CHAPTER TWELVE

Cemetery

I felt as though Catherine was standing next to me, showing me flash cards of dogs, from St. Bernard's, Rottweiler and Jack Russell. Several dog pictures on cards as she waved them like a magician saying "pick a card, any card." I could sense my hand selecting each one that had followed me through my lifetime. I could sense the office and the window I would look out. While lost in self discovery. Feeling individual chains unlock one by one. She gave me the keys and I bravely undid them. I had always admired The Humane Society and wondered if this would be a place to volunteer my time?

With bravery I let all the dogs out in my mind. I freed them from the cage that I had contained them in my mind. One by one I ripped the cards, laughing. Knowing that my family is now gone. Free to roam where they choose and I no longer restricted by that cage labelled weakness.

I secured the crucifix from the dining room table and took the vase with the rose from the kitchen. Without talking to anyone I grabbed my sweater as it was getting cool. I secured Quasar's leash and guided her into the backseat. She was excited, a car ride.

I sent Paul a text message and explained that I loved him and would be home soon. I got a response asking if everything was okay. It was I explained and not wanting him to worry about the dog, I explained she was with me.

I drove through our old neighbourhood when we were kids. Pointing for Quasar and explaining who use to, live in which house. I showed her where my brothers played street hockey and also where we swam at a public pool. The corner store Nick used to buy his cigarettes when he was twelve and the streetlight Philip was caught at when he ran away from home at ten. Sad he was ever found. My dad's morality was strong, even though Philip had broken the rules in the house for stealing money from his wallet. Hmmm habits are hard to break?

There was also the bench on Elm St where Carmen had to sit when he broke his leg and was hobbling to the doctors. Our mother went with him, crying with worry. Our father was at work and couldn't take time off. She didn't even call him, because in that timeframe, this wasn't an option. Your employer owned you. You found out at dinner time.

Quasar seemed interested. Her tail wagged, mostly when the pitch of my voice would rise. I continued pointing out school and churches throughout Evandale, even showed her the office of Mr. Scarpenza. She started to growl and I thought, she really was a smart dog. I turned to look at her and in her excitement I said pointing to the office, "bad boy". I laughed. Determinations by the Law Society would embarrass him. A small town like Evandale would judge. That judgement would nail him financially. Karma was perhaps the bigger bitch I thought. I could hear Quasar's excitement; a cat ran across the road.

We made it to St. Anthony's Cemetery. We came in from the Catholic side. I parked the car and noticed it was just me and the dog visiting this late afternoon. I let Quasar out and she darted after a squirrel. I grabbed my crucifix and rose and left the vase and purse in the car. I wandered first over to my parents, a fresh grave with flowers strewn across fresh dirt. I could see the pageantry of ribbons left to the elements of the weather with ribbons with Mom and Grandma, Aunt and Friend in different colors. Lying across roses, carnations and various funeral flowers, I pondered while I visited. My father's picture still in good standing my mother's yet to be mounted to the tombstone. Perhaps her picture will become the poster for elderly abuse? Her olive skin, her Italian gold earrings and an apron like dress accentuating the joy of cooking. Unsure if those earrings were still in her possession at death? No one could steal from her anymore. I was at peace.

I watched Quasar ecstatically run up and down the cemetery chasing anything that moved. She was so free. No restrictions. No chain. I with crucifix in hand intended to place it in the bronze vase that was chained to the headstone. Some yellow silk flowers were placed there. I thought bronze and yellow would be a nice combination. So I slipped it between the stems of the silk flowers, admiring it like I had just completed a work of art. As I evaluated I could see Quasar by Maria Salmona's sons grave. She was sniffing and exploring. A sense came over me. I turned, resurrecting the crucifix from the bronze vase and with a bit of a skip in my step I made my way to his grave. I placed the bronze cross in his chained vase.

I stood reviewing the art I had contributed. I thought Maria would be delighted on her next trip, seeing that her son had a visitor. She needed lots of healing. She had limited her mobility emotionally for years. She deserved to be free of pain.

I took a few petals from the rose and sprinkled it on his grave. I continued walking and dropping my mothers layers of beauty on familiar graves. We made it to Nick's on the other side of the cemetery, closer to Stanton Hill. I left two remaining petals. I sat on the bench by his site and just thought. I thought of the joy I had just received in the mail. The future was shining with hope. Layers upon layers now peeled back and only the thorns left. I flung the last two petals, knowing that a Rottweiler dominated a lazy bloodhound. A lazy bloodhound couldn't twist stories anymore. I watched them delicately flutter to their resting place, one on Nick's and one on his eternal neighbour, a suicide victim who struggled with bipolar, how calming. Nature had shared the last two indiscriminatingly.

I hoped to see headlines in the local paper soon. I hoped so strong that a thorn again pricked my palm. I heard the six o'clock bells chime in a distance from the church. I thought of Pavlov's dog as I watched Quasar sniffing the grounds. I thought of myself and my conditioned response to fear throughout my life. My inherited restricted range imposed by parents who were chained by their own measures. I trusted that truth would unhitch each link of my fear bound armour. Not just truth of circumstances but truth of who I am to me.

CHAPTER THIRTEEN

Winter

The fall had blown away into the crispness of winter. The snow was both daunting and pretty. The unmarked snow seemed to be a canvass of potential. Potential, until Quasar used the snow for bathroom facilities. The canvass marred by a member of nature. The odd bird would hover about, ever so gently landing, looking for food. A wandering hungry squirrel scattering by, also looking for food. Competition between the two was fierce at times and Quasar liked anything that moved. The killer dog instinct would kick in. Body lowered, back up, legs ready. Her attention was one hundred percent. Truth be told, I am not convinced she'd know what to do with the little guy if her abilities panned out. The mailman however, not sure?

I would drive by the cemetery occasionally over the winter time with the dog, staring at partially visited graves. My parent's grave had no attendees. How surprised? Maria Salmona's son had a winter wreath and small Christmas tree with ornaments. How dedicated her life had become. Thankfully she is retired. My brothers on the other hand had yet to visit our parents. Not one additional footprint, other than Quasar and my own.

I decided to drive by my grandparent's grave and waved from a distance. The snow seemed deeper in that section, as the ground dipped. Quasar was excited in the backseat. A stray cat had wandered into the graveyard. Her reaction was one of excitement, mine of concern. A large golden retriever running from passenger window to passenger window can be annoying. Especially when you know the capture will never happen. The doors have child proof locks, and I had no intention of stopping. As I slowly moved down the roadway seeing the calmness reflected in St. Anthony cemetery as there were no visitors, I had thoughts of concern.

I had yet to hear any news from the Law Society. I guess that old saying "no news is good news" could apply here. My biggest concern however is, would an organization admit to fault finding? Decisions were made by the courts, supported by wrong information? God knows the church has does this, believed false information, or actually created false information. If history repeats itself as it often does, why would my situation be remedied? Would truth prevail and guilty people be revealed? I was holding onto hope that I was worried may be nothing more than a frayed thread.

I remember when The Pope announced in September 2007 that the Knights Templar had not committed an act of heresy. How noble of them to stand on their golden pulpit and admit to this. Even though it did take seven hundred years! God bless them, admission frees the soul. Perhaps the greed of a financially struggling France and deceitful king could render some truth as why innocent people were tortured. How the Grand Master Jacques de Molay who was hunted, caught, tortured for years at Domme prison and wronged by the Pope to whom he answered to. Or rather out manoeuvred by a sinister plan?

No difference I assume than siblings baptized in the same symbolic water? Hmmm, perhaps I do need to be concerned? Most organizations have trouble admitting fault? Doesn't make them look good when they say "Oops"! though.

Well, the fact the exoneration was publicly noted that The Knights Templar, **hadn't** committed heresy is a baby step forward for an Organization that claims the gateway to heaven or hell. Forgiveness for something that was never committed? Something so sinister to be made to look like it was committed? Hmmmm, how ingenious, how family like?

Actually, when Jacques de Molay was crucified, he cursed the Pope and King Philip. His last dying breaths he projected his curse. Within that year the Pope died. Within fourteen years the king of whom he also cursed, his entire lineage was destroyed. Hmmmm, I have heard there is power in words. Perhaps the power is in truth? Perhaps energy packed by truth is displayed like a missile toward wrongdoers?

God help those when that missile gets unleashed and their makeshift cross hangs the burdens of their corruption like dirty laundry hanging out to dry. The soul can't ignore what it's done. Perhaps we are all cursed by our decisions throughout time. A documented history etched in our souls such as the Akashic record?

I wonder if the smell of burning flesh satisfies the pompous ego of throne sitters today. Those who would be nothing without their thrones? How power hungry can a human being be to do unjust things to satisfy a craving of Authority. No different than a dog drooling when it sees a bone? How crippled are we as a community to have figure heads rank our moral souls? Souls ranked by those who have committed immoral acts at that? Are we not capable of Self Reflection or Self Responsibility? It was Confucius that stated "the world would be a clean place if we all swept the stoop in front of our own homes". Why can't we just implement that and be self regulating? But then what would replace Opulent Temples? Real Estate could be plentiful? Perhaps parks where the community could commune?

It seems as a society today we still behave like children on a play ground. Ostracized if we display differences? Knight Templar knocked off the teeter totter so the reigning pope and king can kick sand in a sand box. Anarchy by a mob mind set or a Lord of The Flies setting. When will humankind learn to play fair?

Differences apparently are threatening, but why? Is there such a vengeful God? Whose story is true? Why couldn't The Templar have their devotion? Why had they been judged by the standards of the church? A ranking tier of people wearing big hats judging, how odd?

History alters stories that are told like a global telephone game played at a party. Distortions stretched like a limited rope around an ethereal ball, restrictive and tight. An idea so desperate to find a joining end and it can't. The effort of might to squeeze the idea must, God willing be let go. Allowing a range of movement, free from mental grips of old thinking to move free, undeterred by dogma. I hope The Law Society has a large range of motion when it reviews the information? Waiting Seven hundred years can be a daunting task.

As I drove down the roadway on my way to Nick's grave site, I noticed a car drive through the archway. It was Maria Salmona. Quasar licked me on the side of my face. I noticed Maria had a bouquet of flowers on her dashboard. As we passed by, her eyes didn't even look my way. Her gaze was staring forward as her hands clenched the steering wheel. Focused she was on the snow covered roadway. I on the bird riding on the roof of her car, just sitting there, almost as if it forgot it could fly.

CHAPTER FOURTEEN

Spring

Spring had arrived with all its pleasantries. Flowers were starting to push their way through the earth, showing the rebirth of nature unto itself. The winter felt colder than normal and long. It was time to put the wrath of winter to rest.

There was much to do around the house before heading out to Evandale Central Park.

Ironing was one of the tasks on the To Do List, while listening to the music of Peter Gabriel's greatest hits. A feather duster was resting nearby waiting to be grazed over the coffee table and pictures of my parents, who had been played for fools. Trickery if you will by family, Lack of Ownership by members of the legal system.

I tested the iron by licking the tip of my index finger, something I had seen my mother do for years. The iron was ready for use. I pressed gently with my hands over my wrinkled shirt on the ironing board before spraying it with some water. Earlier I had debated whether or not I should donate it. Seeing how I am a Capricorn, practicality tormented me.

The song San Jacinto bellowed out of the speakers from the family room. I grabbed the feather duster, leaving the iron standing upright and began moving vigorously to the music of Peter Gabriel. I mimicked the artist with my pretend microphone at the chorus. Quasar was running through the house with a sock in her mouth.

Apparently I had dropped it while gathering the laundry. I wanted so desperately to retrieve it from her, but the blast of the guitar and beating drums had me locked in on a pretend stage in between the laundry room and family room. The intensity of the words resonated so deeply that I found myself almost dropping to one knee with an extended hand clasping the air when Paul walked into the room. His bewildered look had immediately broken the mood of the moment. I lowered the duster and continued to just nod my head to the beat, while his eyebrows lowered and his facial expression screamed, what on earth are you doing? Capricorns feel embarrassment when searching for strength. Well, only in the search. When we get it, we venture far.

Quasar dropped the sock and ran quickly toward him jumping up and down. I turned the music off and was wondering what he was doing back already. I retrieved the black sock which had dog fur on it and walked over to give Paul a kiss. "No one show up?" I asked. "Not one "he said. "I did think Calvin would have at least bothered to show up, but guess something must have come up." Calvin was the most loyal to the Masonic brotherhood. He was the historian for the Lodge, replacing his father who passed on.

Quasar was rubbing her head on Paul's thigh. She was loyal, never a doubt. I hid the sock in my pocket so she wouldn't get any ideas. Fifty year olds like myself who are unfit, don't like to run. We do like to sing though. We do appreciate artists like Peter Gabriel who contain hidden wisdom in lyrics.

"After I finish cleaning up around here, I was going to venture out over to Wal-Mart then to the cleaners to drop off your suit for hemming. Want it to be ready for your important day."

"Oh yeah," Paul responded. "Just two weeks away".

"That it is" I responded. "That it is".

"So is the humidity a killer"? I asked Paul. His face a bit red but there was no noticeable sweat. He raised his right hand to wipe a bead of sweat hiding beneath his hairline. "Not bad at all" he responded.

"Looks like it will be a picture perfect day for the Festival with all the festivities at the park. Actually saw one clown, two horses and a grown man dressed like a cowboy. He looked like Woody from Toy Story".

I laughed. Woody was a sharp dresser for a toy cowboy. Mr. Potato head on the other hand, looked more like a car salesman. The most fashionable would be Miss Bo Peep of course. A southern belle if you like. Andy was so lucky to have them all. Every kid should have a menagerie of friends. Adults tend to forget the menagerie and stay stuck between the confines of who do I owe, and how much? Jealousy and judgement run a close second?

Reality can certainly destroy the adult if they are not careful. Ideas of incompleteness, self worth, and comparisons caused by a pull string of negative self talk will eventually deplete the desire to live. Or worse yet, live an unfulfilled life. Perhaps this was my brother's issues?

I pulled the sock from my pocket and thought it wise to throw it into the wash, wanted to at least get that going before vacuuming. I lowered the lid and noticed Quasar following me. Knew it wouldn't be for long because the vacuum would soon be turned on. I was right. A 9 year old dog had not found a way to attack and destroy an upright Eureka. I could hear Paul from the kitchen laughing and then said, "one way to get her out of your way Katia".

I yelled back, "to bad that tail couldn't be put to use. Eliminate some dusting for me". Paul was grabbing a quick sandwich before the lawn needed cutting.

I completed much of the tedious tasks that keep a home looking like a home and not a stable. My shirt was pressed and I re-examined it as I had planned on wearing it today. Diane had donated it. Well she thought she did. I saw it in the bag and grabbed it before she donated her belongings into the donation bin. I thought it sad to say good bye to a shirt that matched a pair of pants I had just bought. Diane wasn't to be blamed for not offering it to me though, she just didn't know about these pants. After all she was only responsible for clearing out her own closets. She wasn't obligated to make sure what my wardrobe had. If only more people cleaned out their closets periodically, perhaps our world would be better place to reside?

I unzipped my knock off Gucci bag and was looking for the laundry tag that I needed to present to the Cleaners so I could pick up my comforter when dropping off Paul's suit. Quasar had thrown up on it. It wasn't her fault though. Perhaps more like mine. Paul was always upset when I snuck her people food. "A dog is a dog Katia, not a human" he would always say. I couldn't debate the facts with him, but he just didn't see how devoted she and I were to each other. I had become her mom by default. Those big eyes always got me, tugged at my heart. Now that the kids were grown and gone I had maintained that spirited energy in the house, how blessed I was. My internal pull string speaks words of happiness, words that erase limiting beliefs.

Frustrated and with much of the contents of my purse on the kitchen table, I knew I had not thrown it out. I fumbled through my wallet. Unzipped a few pockets in the inside lining and turned it over to unsnap a back pouch, nothing. Well not really nothing. I found candy wrappers, a few grocery receipts and the library card I had been looking for. A picture that came with the wallet and my car keys, less the pompom that was attached to the chain. Hmmm, where on earth could I have left it? I stood as my eyes searched deep into my mind retracing the last 48 hours. I knew I had it when I dropped the groceries on the counter. I identified each of the items as I could visually recall taking them out of the bags. From fruit, dairy, cereal and dog treats. I had the round dollar size receipt in my hand. I could see the number on it. Number 279. As I stood trying to capture the memory I heard Paul walk into the entranceway on his way to get something in the closet. "You wouldn't have seen a receipt for the cleaners, number 279 would you?" I asked, while convinced he'd probably say no.

"Is it round, about the size of a loonie"? He responded.

Excitedly I responded, "as a matter of fact, yes, have you seen it?"

"Yes", he stated "I tossed it in the junk drawer the other day. I was going to tell you but forgot. I was cutting that watermelon up and didn't want it to get juice all over it. So I tossed it out of harms way".

I was relieved to hear this. I could continue my day as planned. I put my purse on the counter and walked over to the drawer. It had the remnants of broken toys, dice, lost crayons, a deck of cards, paint strips, keys that belonged to something, a protractor, compass, an eraser, a shoe token from the game Monopoly and finally, the comforter receipt. A round tag with the number 279 in large black ink was buried beneath a small plastic Smurf. The junk drawer had saved the day.

Paul yelled up "how on earth do you remember the number on that tag? Sounding perplexed.

"Easy, its my numbers from the Life Purpose System" I responded. Confused, Paul responded "oh, okay".

I completed my shopping. Wal-Mart had the sale items on the list, hair dye and silk flowers. New arrival of colourful varieties, how visually appealing.

I was happy they had my colour of dye. Going white was not something I anticipated. But after raising a family and looking in the mirror I just knew my inner self was screaming "you need to fix this". Looking good and feeling good was the message of the day. I somehow knew Quasar really didn't care. Oh how I love her. Non judgement is such an amazing quality that so many don't possess.

Both drop off and pick up to the Cleaners were completed. The comforter smelled fresh. The suit dropped off. Special instructions were given to not shrink it. Mrs. Carty always laughed when I teased her. She is an Asian woman that married a local of our community. She spoke some English and was improving all the time. It was quite a different life for her here in Canada. I loved teasing her. She had an infectious smile. They never shrunk anything. Loyal customers appreciate good quality service. They were only hemming the pants.

I placed the comforter in the trunk and headed over to the festival. Sandra was displaying her artwork today. She sent me a text message telling me the town had granted her a booth situated next to the Splash Pad at the southwest section of the park.

This festival had been orchestrated by our town council to bring money into the community. It was comprised of a few blow-up castles, a Ferris wheel, The Zipper, The Whip, a Carousel, a Stage for performances and the other items found at your typical low budget festival, fashioned around the regular park equipment bolted into the ground.

Craft booths and food vendors strewn across the park. It was a hit with people looking for something to do on a weekend when hockey or dance wasn't on the agenda.

I don't mean to imply in a bad way. It just seems that there are those who fill their days with outward pleasure, rather than deep introspection. A clown, a horse and a cowboy for some people make a world of difference.

CHAPTER FIFTEEN

Park

The roadway was blocked off to allow for attendees to roam freely through the downtown core and the park. Vendors were plentiful this year. Ice cream had multiple places for purchase. One was by the balloon guy. You know the guy who can craft a poodle or a dachshund. Next to him was the candle lady. Soy candles, the new fad. Next to her was the oil lady, selling essential oils and Aromatherapy products together. It looks like she has a double venture going on. There was a hotdog vendor, a recruiter for the university, a financial booth offering a range of products and a Tarot card reader. Choice ranges were plentiful. Rather different. Possibly there was something for everyone. The Tarot reader looked the most promising actually. Was wondering if he could tell when the bull market is expected to leave? The financial booth would probably benefit from his services? I laughed trying not to let anyone see. This was the first year a card reader was allowed to participate. Not sure if it was out of financial desperation from the town or if the community was expanding their thinking? Hopefully the Pope wasn't visiting today. After all Evandale for the most part hadn't broadened its perspective beyond the church's dogma. What would it be next, an Astrologer?

I worked my way through the crowds of young parents waiting in lines for food or a ride. I tried to ignore a few guests I knew from my early years. You know those people you don't have anything in common with beside parents. Sometimes those are the ones you need to be most cautious of.

I made it to Sandra's booth. She was sitting closest to the Splash pad which made for good entertainment. There was always a kid who stood right next to the water spout eyeing it in between the timer going off and on and would get blasted with a burst of forced water right in the face. Tears followed and a running parent dumbfounded that their kid had not figured out the mechanics. I must admit, it is funny.

Almost felt obligated to extend a word of endearment like "are you okay?" But I couldn't. The laughter just seemed to take a path of its own. Perhaps the experience could be labelled, a teachable moment?

Sandra was donning a floral smock today, talking to a prospective client. Questions were raised about the type of paints she used and if sketching a family portrait may be a possibility. I sat quietly on a lawn chair waiting, behind the display table looking at my phone. No one was looking for me. Not even Facebook. Not one tag or notification.

Sandra offered me a water bottle as she was getting ready to sit. It appeared that the other booths had far more lines than she had. "How's it been"? I asked. Seeing as there were two small paintings no longer secured to the side of her press board wall.

"Not bad" she responded. "Could be better, I guess. Glad this isn't my day job." We both laughed. Being an artist has always had the inference of being a starving profession. It appeared wealth is achieved after death, when the value increased. Not quite sure in Sandra's case, that's going to be a factor? But it was a hobby and hobby's help with expression. The jewellery booth seemed like it had the advantage. Who didn't like fake gems that sparkle? Birthstones were always a hit. Most people knew their astrological sign and birthstone. I know this because I once worked in a jewellery store. Seemed odd though that the thought of characteristics from their birth sign contributed to personality traits? Was it not Shakespeare that said "the fault lies not in the stars but within ourselves?" Hmmm.

How odd, yet how many people search out to know more about themselves? Horoscopes are still published in the daily paper. The internet has infinite number of sites that advertise numerology and astrological reports. Books are written every year on the subject. Several of these entertainers / visionaries make their way to television. Is it a scam? Or are we just poor suckers so desperate to know who we are? I recall Catholic school teaching us "to thy own self be true". So if people were searching to know more about themselves, was this so wrong?

Perhaps the Church should have its own booth here today. Recruiting like the University for enrolment. After all there are plenty of religions competing for our souls. The Army makes men out of boys, or at least give them a truer depiction of what mankind is really like? Perhaps the neighbouring property should have a Symposium on this? Booths placed in a circular fashion on the Museum grounds. After all, both Religion and Museums contain a history with relics of the past.

I can almost visualise it. The Catholics, directly across from the Protestants. The Hindu's across from The Buddhists. The Evangelical across from the Taoist, Jainism across from Islam. The Agnostic across from The Atheist and New Age across from Pentecostal. We would need twelve booths, six to the left, six to the right of a central booth. Not like DaVinci's last supper. That was too linear, that feels more like the head table at a wedding. This would be more circular. To show how the inclusion of the differences perfect the circle. Just need to figure who the central character would be in the center booth, perhaps ourselves?

Was religion even necessary? Was the very existence of religion just habit forming, addictive in nature? Removing it creating a void? A void that encompassed fear and a fear so unfathomable that the creation of a devil, hoofed and looking dehydrated, cast in black tights, accentuated with a pitchfork became the role model? Hmmm, no wonder Astrology has always appealed to me. Let's face it; absurdity is just that, religion I mean.

I saw the clown walking by with a bunch of colourful balloons all held together with ribbons. His painted on smile was so well done. He was a middle aged man earning extra cash. Being laid off from the factory can certainly hurt a family. God had no doubt provided. He certainly livened up a group of kids with free balloons, that's for sure. Kids ran to him with no filters. It's not their fault really; John Wayne Gacy was generations before them. Killer clowns often times look like the rest of the crowd. So do abusers? So how are we supposed to know who the bad guys really are? Hmmmm. Where does one turn for spiritual discernment?

The afternoon had been predictable in nature. People were wandering about having a pleasant time. Not what I would describe as noteworthy, but pleasant. It filled a void for anybody looking for a free admission event. Children laughed. Children cried. Adults spent money, vendors smiled. The world of commerce evolved. As Sandra and I caught up on events happening in our lives we gossiped more than perhaps we should have. But in our defence, it made us feel good about ourselves. We were just taking a tally on whose marriage was in trouble or whose children were announcing gender issues? Seemed that Truth in families was becoming more acceptable, in the twenty first century or at least society was embracing acceptance, or rather being forced to at least review it.

See we weren't making fun of people, we were stating the obvious predictions from years ago. We had our feelings about who was getting married for the right reasons when we were younger. We both had a weight problem and had an added advantage. We could see things from a different platform. See when you live your life from a distance, lack of acceptance keeps you far enough away that you can see the real reasons people do what they do. See Catholic school had given me a high seat on the bleachers early on in life. Being a spectator of the sport we would describe as life. See, the doctrine taught was contradictory. Do unto others was just a phrase. Build your house on rock, not sand. Just passing phrases is all they were. Perhaps the literal interpretation is what our classmates and teachers thought?

Symbolism or metaphors eluded many. One nun was rumoured to be reassigned to another school. She had had a baby. Father Murray had been a player apparently.

God had blessed me. Not in the traditional way, through religion or worship. The Wizard of Oz had fallen in my hands. Not literally. I don't mean to suggest I was walking down the street and then suddenly from the sky a book fell. That tale was Chicken Little. Well sort of. See L. Frank Baum was a thinker that's for sure. Several other stories hidden on library shelves can certainly shine a light toward intelligence, if you're searching though? False hoods and self importance can fall hard. Hard into the depth of a pretend Hell named after a Norse God Hella. A myth, hijacked. A myth used to bring terror to the stage of life. How interesting as libraries hold so much history. Perhaps the Museum and Library should be united?

How blessed Dorothy Gale from Kansas was on her journey. A journey of herself to herself. Sad that Aunt Em and Uncle Henry were afraid of the law. We could all tell they didn't want to give up Toto. They were upstanding God fearing, law fearing, citizens. They didn't want to defy it even though Aunt Em had issues with Elvira Gulch. Perhaps her church never told her **fear** is a blinding curtain? That empowerment comes from a journey on the road of Life.

Sandra and I had had a pleasant afternoon together. I thanked her for the water and knew we would reconnect in the near future. I know this because this had always been our routine. When I hugged her and said goodbye, I could see the Tarot reader across the way and thought I would leave the park by walking past the booth. Two kids running toward the ice cream booth almost tripped me. My thoughts were unkind, but no one fell. I walked at a decent pace looking at the crowd, evaluating the success of the day. There was no doubt, the local Gazette will highlight the day in their next publication. A photo of a kid standing next to the clown, eating an ice cream as mom and dad watch in the distance. A perfect emotional marketing ploy. This photo will set the stage for next year. Planning is the key.

I made it the Tarot Tent and looked over the items spread across the display table. There were several decks of cards being sold, from Angel decks to regular decks. Pendulums to crystals and a fee chart with a list to write your name for a reading. This was in case there was a wait. I noted the list of names that had been scratched off. Mr. Tarot reader was at the back of his tent reading someone as I was gazing over his products. Was he a charlatan like the Wizard, or a man of divinity and wisdom? Perhaps a 30 minute reading would evidence this? I jotted my name down, Katia Secord, looked at my watch and was interested to know what the seer knew. But it needed to go quick because I had to make dinner. The time was four thirty.

A tall thin young lady walked out, laughing with the Seer as she thanked him. I expected him to kiss her hand and speak in a French accent. He didn't. He was a regular middle aged man that looked like Mark Twain. Thanked her for coming by and she parted ways. The smile on her face, lead me to believe she is either getting married, pregnant or coming into money? Unfortunately I would never know. Mr. Twain reviewed the pending list and looked me in the eye and called "Katia Secord"! I was the only person standing, waiting, so the deduction had not been difficult. But to his credit, some people note their name and run. I nodded and he returned the greeting. "So, you are in want of a Tarot reading?" he asked. "There are several formats you can opt for. There is a 5 minute, a 15 minute and a 30 minute reading. Here are the price ranges." He handed me a list. I gazed over it and chose 30 minutes for thirty dollars. I was splurging. "Oh and by the way please sign this waiver form?" He gracefully included in the paper below the list of names. Legal jargon, exempting him from repercussions. Perhaps the psychic world had some legal hurdles yet? Perhaps pregnancies and wealth had not arrived on indicated time frames? Hmmm.

I was invited into a back room with a curtain dividing the front section of the tent, a small area with a wicker table and chairs. Mr. Twain sat first and removed any confusion as who was to sit where.

He stared at me for a few minutes while reaching for a deck of cards. Immediately I recognized the deck. They were the Rider deck. I owned this pack. I smiled and whimsically he noticed my excitement and asked "you seem familiar with these?" He held them up displaying them proudly.

"I am", I uttered," I have owned three of these decks in my life time."

"And your thoughts on them" he inquired?

"Mixed feelings, really". I responded.

"You're not a believer?" He asked.

"Define believer?" I responded.

"A believer of the natural forces of nature?" He queried.

"Divine force?" I asked.

"Where the presence of intentions are driven into a power house of direction, driven by you to magically play itself out into the future, granting you what you have been focusing on, Either for good or for bad?" He responded.

"Then Yes" I answered.

He grabbed the deck and put it back into the box. I was puzzled at his reaction. He sat staring at me and I at him. Nothing was said. I found myself listening to the sound of balloons popping, smelling kettle corn. What was Mr. Twain doing I thought?

After a pause, Mr. Twain asked me directly, "what are you really doing here?"

Unsure as why he didn't want my money, I spoke up and said "I want you to give me a reading?"

"No you don't," he responded. "That's why I put the deck away. See people who don't understand how the force of nature works look to the tarot for direction. But that's not why you're here?"

I was at a loss for words. This doesn't happen often. My face felt red and sweaty. I had been caught.

"I don't get too many like you in here", he responded. "Most often I am inundated with tell me when I will win the lottery? When will I get married? How many kids will I have?"

haunt us? Maybe someone awakened the war of years ago by walking into a time warp or energy field?"

Mark Twain laughed. "You are aware of energy fields?"

"I am" I responded. Thinking that this really wasn't the case, but I certainly was aware of them.

"You are an interesting person Katia Secord" mentioned Mr. Twain.

"How so" I responded.

"Well, most people today are trying to sort out a career that will bring them happiness. Where to go on vacation or should I have kids or not?

Not energy fields, time warp or Tarot cards that are not fortune telling tarot cards at all?

I looked into Mr. Twain's eyes and felt humbled. An old soul recognized another.

As I stared at Mr. Twain and extended a hand for a formal introduction, I admitted to him how his exterior presence was very similar to Mr. Twain. He laughed and stated that he got that a lot. So playing with this idea, I asked "since Haley's comet hasn't been around again, your really not him are you?"

He laughed, but unconvincingly. He went on to say "my name is Samuel Lewis Clairmont." And officially shook my hand.

I wasn't sure if the universe had so well crafted his name or his parents intuited the initials of their son decades earlier?

I smiled. He smiled. "Have a seat, he suggested, but not in the tent. Let's sit on that picnic table." He pointed to the empty table with wrappers leftover from some family's lunch. A water bottle left on its side was blowing back and forth from a gentle breeze. A kid ran by and stepped on his pop can making it into a shoe. I laughed. I hadn't seen a kid do that in years.

Mr. Clairmont gathered the garbage and walked over to a garbage bin, slightly overflowing. He jammed the contents as best he could into the opening of the bin, trying to ignore the stench. Gently brushing his hands along his pant legs, while walking over toward me. The mishap in the distance was still carrying on but with less enthusiasm. People trained would take care of the event. No doubt. I pointed to the kid running with the can on his foot and jokingly said, "he looks like Tom Sawyer". We both got a chuckle out of that.

I sat on the opposite side of the picnic table looking at the carvings etched into Town property. Apparently lovers had once felt something. Question was did they still? There was a carved heart with an arrow listing the names of Mark & Dave with a random date of ten yeas ago. I dragged my finger across the etching and stated "I wonder how Mark's life unfolded? Mr. Clairmont agreed. "Perhaps persecuted by people who have their own hidden truths, no doubt, isn't that the way it always is"?

I was feeling a kindred spirit with Mr. Clairmont and nodded.

"So what brings you to the festival today Katia?" He asked.

"Well I promised my girlfriend I would stop by and say hi." I pointed with my left arm toward the southerly part of the park. "If you stretch your neck and lift yourself off of the bench, you can see she is the one selling paintings."

He gracefully followed my instruction and could indeed see her from a distance. "Oh how nice" he suggested. "Are you here for anything else?"

I wasn't quite sure at what he meant by this. So I inquired, "like…?.."

"Like…?.." he responded.

I felt as though I couldn't hide anything from myself anymore. See I understood the Laws of Attraction more and more each day. Watching the events I was attracting to myself, lost in the beauty of its own design. Energy with creative vigour is like a painter who paints uninhibited by an audience. Beauty splashes intently into a unique design. I was searching for direction, or rather, approval.

"Approval, ….yeah that's what I am looking for" I nodded and nodded reaffirming my own direction.

"From?" He responded.

"Well, that would be me". I knew this no doubt.

"So why then, the need for a reading from a stranger with a deck of cards"? Mr. Clairmont asked.

I smiled, I think I knew the answer and I knew that he knew the answer. Not sure how?

We stared at each other. Nothing needed to be said. My phone dinged.

Paul needed me home, the text read. Company had arrived. Oh and you have mail, important mail.

I stood. Mr. Clairmont did not. He was watching the ambulance attendees cart someone off on a gurney. Whispers circled as people walked passed. Terrorism was the new word of the day. Uneasiness was brewing. The young ambulance attendee confirmed, firecracker misfire. Fake news has more impact.

CHAPTER SIXTEEN

Letter

Quasar loved company. Not just any company, but company that brings treats. Paul's Masonic brother Gordon was coming by. A first degree was impending and both wanted to sharpen their memory work after a good meal. Both had been past Master's and had some memory work to help a new initiate with his commitment to The Craft. Freemasonry held a deep rooted lineage in Paul's family. They were men who have prided themselves for living their lives by the square and compass. Centuries of Secords that date back to Scotland. Date back to a time period secrets were kept for a reason. People were being killed for disclosing truths. Truths that DaVinci so desperately sought out to understand himself. A forward thinker, whose creative ideas were attempted to be inhibited by dogmas and tradition, victimized by the time period and restricted of his true self, by those who had been locked into a mental darkness, afraid of progress. Suppressing his genius, while battling an authority trying to make him wrong? The Church no less, an organization that didn't embrace the divinity within the man but rather tormented the soul he inherited.

Perhaps a man that used his left hand was not cursed by a devil, but blessed by a quantum intelligence that was etched within his very soul. As it is in each and everyone of us! This knowingness stitched into our cells, dancing with a knowledge of who we really are, trying to reveal itself to itself, like a Kansas girl on a journey to discover that she really didn't need to venture beyond her own back yard. Why had the church been so crippling? Why are generations so limiting? Why, why, oh why, is the fear so strong!

Paul walked over to the door just before the doorbell rung. He wanted to keep Quasar at bay before she would fly down the hallway at a maddening speed to greet Gordon. Too late, the damage was done. A big boned golden retriever was in excitement mode going full throttle toward a glass door. "Oh my, oh my" Paul nervously said, trying to get between the dog and the door. Gordon entered, trapped between the screen door and the glass door with Paul extending his left leg like a barricade. Fortunately, Gordon was no stranger.

With the grand entrance and a treat, the commotion digressed to a smelling of shoes at the door. Paul and Gordon shook hands and Paul welcomed him into the family room. "Did you go to the festival today" Paul asked Gordon.

"No, hadn't the time, been working on the motorcycle. Want to get the bike back on the road."

When I arrived home I was excited to see Gordon. Being a widower had not devastated him nor prevented him from moving forward with his life. We hugged, and sat for a visit. Losing a wife to cancer had been enough.

Paul went to grab a couple of beers, and mentioned, "You might want to open that letter sitting on the table", while staring at me with raised eyebrow and a flick of his chin. Suddenly a sick feeling came over me. Quasar followed me. I decided to walk by the envelopes stacked. With some curiosity I hesitated. Quasar sniffed the envelopes as though he was employed at the airport. A growl ensued. He had the right reaction, it was the hydro bill. But better yet, a response from The Law Society. My hands were sweating, my heart racing, Quasar sniffing like there was food in the envelope. I had to sternly tell her to back off. However, I proceeded to pat her on the head; after all she is my friend.

Gordon looked at me perplexed as I was quieter that usual. "You okay Katia" he asked concerned? I began reading. My hands shaking, my throat feeling tense surprised at the words. I turned over the first page, the second page with more force. The third page I dropped and just stood there. Quasar growled.

CHAPTER SEVENTEEN

Fireworks

The fireworks were going to start at 10:05 p.m. exactly. According to the Schedule and how The Event Co-ordinator has operated in year's past. First boom of excitement will introduce the "Ooooo's" and "Awwwww's" by all age groups. I knew I wanted to see them, but truth be told, I wanted to see Mr. Clairmont before the park closed. Paul had indicated to me that he would meet me on The Museum grounds, by the large Oak tree. This tree has been the meeting ground for the last twenty five years. Sandra would bring the blanket and set-up camp there when she closed her booth. This was such a lovely spot. The back of The Museum grounds that borders The River. It seemed so surreal, with its picturesque quality of broken islands in the distance.

I got to the park and checked my watch, it was eight o'clock. Still ample time before booths shut down. Closing time was nine thirty, according to the entry sign. The crowd seemed to have disbursed, either toward the Museum just adjacent or wandering about the town. Sidewalk sales were going on and cafes were set up for stragglers and tourists.

I picked up my pace looking to see if there was any familiar faces, or any remnants from the horse that was offering rides for a dollar. Manoeuvring is a skill not just with public events but life really. I was feeling that right now and needed to talk to Mr. Clairmont.

I could see him at a distance. He had a book in his hand, standing, looking toward the westerly sunset over the river. A woman stood next to him. A big busted woman dressed in historical garments. She appeared to be one of the members for the re-enactment from the Museum. At least I hoped, otherwise she wandered into the wrong time period. Google needed to do a search to find her time frame so she can return home. I snickered to myself. I checked to see if Sandra's booth was still open. From a distance I could see her standing motioning with her hands something to a customer. Could be a sale?

I neared Mr. Clairmont and coughed just behind him. Both he and the historical woman turned. Delighted he was to see me, and extended his hand. "Katia he said, you've come back". I had hoped he'd kiss my hand like the gentleman that he appeared to be, but he didn't and still no French accent. The woman turned and looked at me with a peculiar look. Mr. Clairmont uttered "Katia, this is my student. She extended her hand and with intensity, squeezed it. She needed some coaching on femininity. "Hi, I'm Marta, so nice to meet you,"

"Hello" I responded, "Nice to meet you as well."

I turned my head, perplexed that Mr. Clairmont had mentioned she was his student and with curiosity asked, "student? You're a student of Mr. Clairmont?"

"Yes, she responded. I am completing my Psychology degree."

"Psychology, I queried, intrigued".

"Yes, with a minor in Theology", was her response.

How divine this truly was. Not just for me but for the three of us. I almost felt a joke coming on. Sometimes anxiety gets the best of me when I giggle to myself. When the universe does synchronistic things like this, I get silly. I almost caught myself saying, A historic woman, Mark Twain and a stranger meet in a park"? But I didn't. I almost did. But I didn't'.

"So, why are you dressed in character Marta"? I asked.

She responded, "Two reasons, one to pay for a student loan the other to document human behaviour."

"Really, I asked"

"Yes." She answered.

Mr. Clairmont could see I was like a fortune teller trying to pry for more information and he asked, "Is that not okay with you, he laughed".

"Oh yes," I said, stumbling on my words. "Just wasn't expecting a Tarot Card Reader to be a professor at a University."

"Why is that odd?" He questioned.

Realizing that I didn't know why I thought it was odd. Other than I was like everyone else assuming that people needed to look and behave a certain way.

That Moment I had realized a core weakness.

Stumbling on my own words, I spoke up nervously saying, "I don't have an answer for you." My face was feeling hot.

They both noticed and Marta spoke up, while looking at Mr. Clairmont and said, "Should we note that". She laughed. He laughed than said "No, predictable is all it was. After all that's what we are studying isn't it?"

Marta nodded with some vigour. Her floral bonnet wasn't tied tightly.

Mr. Clairmont spoke up, looking me in the eye and asked, "Are you here for the fireworks?"

"I am, I spoke up. "My husband is meeting me at The Museum grounds. We will be watching them with our friend."

He nodded looking at me and asked "was there anything else?"

My inner being must have amplified confusion with my nervousness and perspiration. There was something I was looking for, help. Help to understand society. Help to understand myself. My biggest fear was, that I already knew, just didn't act on it.

First and foremost though, why is a Professor of Psychology doing research on vulnerable people at a social event?

I cleared my throat while searching for something to say. Impulsively I spewed "Why are you doing this?

Mr. Clairmont snickered but not demeaning. He spoke up and said, "You came to my booth remember?"

He was right. No one lured me there. Curiosity had gotten the better of me. His lack of pursuing me was another startling characteristic that bothered me.

"Perhaps you met your own internal crossroad?" Marta said.

"What do you mean?" I questioned, feeling that her dated look was more reflective of an old soul.

"See Mr. Clairmont spoke very highly of you when I met up with him. In fact he was intrigued that you were not desperately searching for something that many people are. "I nodded feeling complimented.

"However, you are searching for something, or the booth would have not visually enticed you. It's that enticement that resonates within you isn't it?"

When she said this, my heart pounded. I wasn't sure why? Something resonated at a deeper level within me, stirring up debris of something left behind.

I stood like a deer in the headlights thinking. There was something that I was fascinated with by the booth. Or rather what it offered. I pondered what felt lake an eternity. A balloon popped startling me. That instantaneous jolt got me to awaken from a trance and asked "Can I get some advice?"

Mr. Clarirmont asked, "You mean from me and Marta or from the cards?"

"Well not the cards, I didn't bring money." We both laughed I was being cynical. I continued, "you know how we talked earlier about divine force?'

Mr. Clairmont nodded. "Yes".

I continued, "Well I feel that the force was kinked up and I need help understanding why?"

"Okay" he responded. "Kinked up exactly how?"

"Well", I started, "I understand about intuition and I am a student of quantum enfoldment in as far as the new information made available to the public is. I am a devote reader and a devote student to observation. My question to you is this, if you had a gut feeling about something, and it turns out to be accurate, but you're angry that its accurate, do you hate yourself for intuiting it, or react that the outcome wasn't what you really wanted?"

Mr. Clairmont tilted his head to the left, Marta to the right. Both thinking of a response. Marta looked at her teacher and stated, "Let me respond if you're good with that?"

Mr Clairmont smiled and nodded with approval.

"So let me get this straight" Marta started. "So to simplify, you got what you expected!"

"Yes" I responded and I am pissed to say the least.

"At who?" Marta responded.

"At the Law Society, they stated in a letter to me that due to the complication of the legal process and the fact that I had a lawyer who was obligated to his profession to deal with these issues and claims that he had, there is nothing more that can be done!" My heart was pounding, my face red. My incompetent lawyer was being acknowledged as a dutiful officer of the court when he had not been. Protected by an organization, that sponsors his license, no different than a church looking the other way when a man is burned at the stake.

Marta responded by saying "breathe Katia, breathe.

I did just that.

My phone dinged and I took a quick second to look at who was sending me a message. It was Paul asking where I went, with a few questions marks.

Still breathing and feeling less of an urge to hurt something, I noticed a grown man playing a cowboy. It was Woody from Toy Story. I was lost for words momentarily and sat on the picnic table I sat on earlier. I was sitting on the bench with my back to the table

it all together. A system established like a magic show in a park. Some understand the trick while the masses walk away lost in the manoeuvre. There are few Woody's in the real world who love the art of entertaining and do the right thing, unfortunately. A cowboy with true dignity can be encouraging.

Sandra arrived with her golden retriever Maverick. Quasar was excited. It was play time. I brought lunch out to the back fenced yard and the two dogs had noticeably missed each other. They were siblings and had similar personalities, lovingly childlike. As the dogs reminisced with rolling on the grass and sniffing the yard Sandra and I sat to the music of Peter Gabriel, some sandwiches and tea. We discussed family issues, pending high school reunions, future weddings and death. Our friendship was like a tapestry that had embroidery of events so delicately sewn to reveal its charm. We matched in colour, we matched in detail. Much of our memories had been shared. We did some tea readings for each other. A skill we gained with practice for thirty years. She has two bells together I noticed. Perhaps, a wedding for her daughter in her future is pending? I have a sword on the rim of my cup. She thought perhaps a victory of some sort?

I heard my phone ding and noticed I received a message from Paul, as Sandra was heading out. The event was a success. New Grand Master installed. I was happy for Paul being able to attend the event. Mingling with hundreds of similar minded souls is warmth to the soul. His love of Masonry and his dedication to the Craft enhanced his life as an upright human being. Something so many fall short on today. I know this because of the amount of people I had seen on the court dockets while being dragged through the system. But then again, how many were treated fair? I thought of Jacques de Molay the Grand Master from 1307. Tortured and burnt like a human steak by a supposed upright organization. I felt my anger intensify. I could hear the wood burn and almost smell the charred remnants of a man undeserving of the repercussions of greed. I immediately tidied up and grabbed Quasar. I assisted her into the backseat of the car and headed out. I drove with anger in my heart and anger in my soul.

Quasar sat looking out the window. Two treats in a day was great. Play time, now a car ride. Could it get any better for a dog, a nap perhaps?

The debris of being made to be wronged and forced to accept authoritative decisions was challenging for me. The debris of assault and no forgiveness was taunting. I entered the grounds of the cemetery from The Protestant section, Stanton Hill. I was on my way to see my parents when I felt compelled to stop in this section. The non compliant heathen that I have so willingly become stopped the vehicle and opened the car door standing at the plot of a neighbour's son who had committed suicide. A young father, lost in direction with life, so many years ago. Raised by a single parent who had intended on being a good parent but resolved her inner struggle with the idea that she did the best she could. Her intentions were never ill directed. His actions should bear no blood on her hands. Sad, that he is divided from Maria Salmona's child in the garden of eternity. Young men, who in their prime were taken from this reality, now united somewhere where divisions are non existent.

Quasar was eager to be free. I opened the door for her and watched her spirited self run. Envious at her enjoyment of life and how simple her world was. Her free soul not hinged by confusion of debris unresolved, other than the mailman. I turned looking around the cemetery as though I was having Vertigo. The dividing lines of eternal rest combined with the unsettling massacre of good people slaughtered by ego driven titled men, had my blood pressure soar. I screamed out in the quietness of the cemetery *"make this right! Hold all those accountable for their actions of ill will! If there is a God, make it known!*

With the vigour of my intention and the release of the ability to direct an outcome I sat on a nearby bench. I felt the warmth of the direct sun and felt better. I felt like a weight was lifted from my shoulders, my emotional self, and my soul. I picked up a stick and tossed it for Quasar. She chased it.

Seasons had come and gone as the sun chased the snow and the snow chased the rain, I made a decision to free myself that day. That day when I turned to the invisible forces of time like Jacque de Molay and released the pressures of knowing the truth. I put the outcome into the hands of the universe to recreate the fragments of distorted facts and restore that truth for visibility. The hope and faith that nature's intelligence would sort the twisted versions in its majestic fashion and like the final scene of a Broadway show, reveal All intentions of those involved, merged and displayed before the curtain draws to a close.

I made a decision to become absorbed into my own life and discard unnecessary mental holds on my past. I established new friendships with spouses from the Lodge and in the community. I volunteered my time with kids who struggled with reading and became active with The Rainbow Girls. I became self employed and enjoyed all the good that was in my life. I took a tally and noticed that there were more pleasantries than that which had burdened me. Being helpful always brought pleasant feelings. A reward that is difficult to explain. I concluded I had done the best I could in fighting against those whose identity hinge on hiding their true self. A mask that falls can ruin many lives. Not only the one who wears it but also those who identify with it.

Eleven months later my phone rang. Excited to see Sandra's name on the call screen I answered with a playful "hello". Immediately I was asked to sit. Laughing, thinking this was a game, I stated "you sit". With a much more serious tone she insisted, so I did.

I had just woken and told her I at least need to grab a cup of coffee. She waited but I could hear a few sighs. Once the mug was filled to my comfort level, I pulled out a chair and sat. "Go," I said laughing. "All ready."

"Have you heard the news this morning?" She queried.

I hadn't. The alarm radio kicked on but I was more concerned about the weather as I was hoping to take a stroll over to the cemetery to place roses on my parents and Nick's grave if weather permitted. "Well "she stated "I am just going to say it because I don't want to beat around the bush. There was a bad car crash by the court house."

"Okay" I said so what does this have to do with me?" I was worried for a moment she was going to say I was to blame. But I shook my head and thought that, that was fear mongering from my old scared self.

Sandra continued. "Your brother Philip was travelling behind his lawyer on the way to the court house when there was a crash. It was Mr. Scarpenza's fault. He's dead and your brother burned in the car behind him. He rammed into him. Your brother was travelling to close and too fast." Carmen had a heart attack when he heard the news!

I sat in shock watching the steam lift off my morning coffee. A few drops slipped onto my hand as I firmly gripped the cup. I felt the burn. I dropped the phone and walked over to the sink and washed my hands. A tear fell from my right eye landing in the sink. I watched the clockwise swirl of the running water wash it down the drain. Time had stood still. I looked out the window and saw the bright rising sun listening to the faint call from Sandra from the distant phone. Katia, Katia.

THE END
Alice Kaycee

ABOUT THE AUTHOR

Alice Kaycee is a 58 year old first generation Canadian and the daughter of parents who braved the journey for a new life from Italy to Canada in the 1950's. As a young child I witnessed the discomfort of watching the need for inclusion as well as the desire to stay connected to traditional ways. The hold so tightly held in the early years eventually loosened and a new place to live was had. However, belief systems that were challenged were so difficult to shed and more often than not, were adhered to without any foundation to hold onto, other than it was a learned behaviour.

I have been living with a diagnosis of Multiple Sclerosis for over thirty years. This diagnosis posed an opportunity to re-evaluate life and examine the substance of what I deem to be important. By being stopped in my tracks by this diagnosis, I became willing to re-examine life patterns. I have become the reflection of what an illness does not have to be, if one chooses wellness. I dedicated my life to removing the chains of restrictions from an identity hinged on limitations, the need for acceptance and the need for approval.

I bravely ventured beyond the world of tradition and desire to learn from various groups of people by just watching. I entered the esoteric world of self discovery as a teenager, much to the dismay of several. I am so grateful to have found and continue to find parts of myself that longs to see the depth of my soul, others soul and the intentions that lie beneath. That area where the TRUTH is the grip that holds the threads of our being together and the threads of our decisions, revealing our choices and displaying our journey to ourselves and to the world.

Alice Kaycee

Printed in the United States
By Bookmasters